Andrew Jackson
and the
Search for Vindication

James C. Curtis

Andrew Jackson
and the
Search for Vindication

Edited by Oscar Handlin

 LONGMAN

An imprint of Addison Wesley Longman, Inc.

New York • Reading, Massachusetts • Menlo Park, California • Harlow, England
Don Mills, Ontario • Sydney • Mexico City • Madrid • Amsterdam

LIBRARY OF CONGRESS CATALOG CARD NO. 75-26427

ISBN 0-673-39334-8

99 00 PAT 20 19

PRINTED IN THE UNITED STATES OF AMERICA

to
Richard W. Leopold
and
Thomas L. Philpott
with respect and gratitude

Editor's Preface

THE SOUTH CAROLINA FRONTIER, the region of Andrew Jackson's birth in 1767, was representative of the nation he led as president sixty years later. Neither wholly southern nor wholly northern, the area was the product of the incomplete fusion of two strains of settlement. Here people from the plantation society of the seaboard met the land-hungry farmers coming down from the mountains. The encounter of the two population movements imparted a raw, western quality to the society in which Jackson grew up. Furthermore he, like many people around him was Scotch-Irish, a member of a restless group, inured by repeated transplantations to hardship and conflict and drawn to the frontier by suspicion of outsiders. And to compound the difficulties of youth in this environment, this was the scene of bitter fighting during the Revolutionary War.

Childhood experience here fastened on Jackson attributes characteristic of the whole nation in the early nineteenth century. Those qualities made him chief executive in 1828 and markedly influenced the two terms he served in the White House.

The United States, after all, was also a product of heterogeneous strains of settlement; it too had only incompletely adjusted to its situation. The blustering self-confidence and disregard of the sensibilities of others that critics ascribed to Jackson were traits he shared with many Americans, as were the predilection for violence and the tendency toward exaggeration. Certainly the insistence upon having one's own way and the willingness to use force in getting it contributed to the outbreak of the War of 1812 in which Jackson gained national prominence; the same characteristics entered into the subsequent assault on the frontier along its whole length. To a considerable extent, these personal and national traits were elements in the phenomenal growth of the United States during Jackson's lifetime. Expansion—territorial, economic, cultural, and social—absorbed goodly amounts of individual aggression.

Imperfect knowledge was also characteristic of the time and place. The country and Jackson stabbed ineffectually at the economic problems of transportation, the currency, and manufacturing, saved from the consequences of error by the healing capacity for growth. All the while, the still greater problem of slavery remained hidden until well after Jackson's death.

An incisive and dramatic analysis of the personality of Andrew Jackson enables Professor Curtis to tell the story of a complex life and also to describe the coming of age of the United States.

OSCAR HANDLIN

Author's Preface

HIS SOLDIERS CALLED HIM Old Hickory, thus commending him to the ages. In the rhetoric of presidential politics, few titles are so vivid, so suggestive of vigor and action. Strength, toughness, physical courage, perseverance—these are qualities we associate with Andrew Jackson and have come to expect in both his martial and presidential successors. Indeed, Jackson ranks among the greatest of American generals and as the first modern chief executive. Always his image is one of action, decisiveness, and determination.

Andrew Jackson was more than a symbol; he was a vital force. As the force was rarely at rest, so the man was rarely at peace. Beneath the aggressiveness, the boldness, the quick temper, lay deep uncertainties rooted in his precarious back country upbringing and in events that left him an orphan at the age of fourteen. Throughout life he felt a need to prove himself, to triumph over enemies he believed were assaulting his reputation. Even in victory, he never felt victorious. The more his reputation grew, the more he feared that some conspiracy, some cabal was working to diminish his standing with the people.

Confronted by death at an early age, Andrew Jackson spent his life trying to prove his right to survival. This quest profoundly influenced his own destiny and that of the nation. Jackson's personal correspondence reveals an intense inner turmoil. I have tried to understand the nature and origins of this emotional turbulence, for it affected all his major decisions whether as frontier general, treaty negotiator, party leader, or chief executive. To overlook these feelings is to miss the essence of the man and the basis for his popular appeal.

Americans expect too much of their heroes and heroines, crediting them with extraordinary feats and superhuman powers. Andrew Jackson confronted such unrealistic expectations in his own lifetime. Hailed as a New World Napoleon, he was nevertheless forced to play the role of Cincinnatus, to lay down the sword and return peacefully to the plow. Selected as standard-bearer for a new political coalition, he had to maintain silence even in the face of vicious campaign slanders. Sworn to defend the presidency from congressional assault, he was at the same time expected to guard against any increase in executive power. Jackson never resolved these dilemmas; quite the contrary, they only magnified his inner tensions.

While often critical of the hero, I have tried to be sympathetic to the man. To recognize that Andrew Jackson was troubled, that he feared death, that his emotions ran to extremes may diminish his reputation as demigod but not as human being. And it is this fundamental humanity that we must affirm if we are to have respect for the past and for our own ability to deal with the insecurities of the present.

I would like to thank a number of institutions for their generous assistance. The University of Delaware provided travel funds for a research trip to Nashville, where the staffs of the Tennessee State Library and the Andrew Jackson Papers Project helped me locate vital, unpublished correspondence. I completed my writing while on leave as a fellow of the National Endowment for the Humanities. My particular thanks go to Carol Schoenherr for her expert typing.

Friendly persuasion, incisive criticism, expert editorial review—I have been fortunate to receive all of these in my work. Professor Peter Carroll encouraged me to pursue this personal biography and helped me analyze Jackson's character. I am extremely grateful for the thought-provoking comments he made on several drafts of the manuscript. Michael Rogin graciously allowed me to read the manuscript of his recently published work on Jackson and the subjugation of the American Indians. Although we differ in our views of Old Hickory's personality, I found Professor Rogin's analysis of Indian affairs suggestive and enlightening. George Basalla, J. Joseph Huthmacher, David Cox, John Andrew, and Steve Schoenherr took time from their own labors to help me in mine. I would also like to thank Oscar Handlin for his invaluable editorial advice. His suggestions and comments have improved the manuscript significantly. All publishers should be blessed with sensitive and thoughtful editors like Marian Ferguson.

Above all, I am grateful to close friends for guidance and support. Professor Richard R. Beeman reviewed the first three chapters of the manuscript and shared with me his extensive knowledge of eighteenth-century American society. His historical judgment is always reliable; mercifully, his backhand is not. Professor Sydney Nathans has been a constant source of encouragement at all stages of this project. By being the most uncompromising of critics, he has been the best of friends. My wife Elisabeth helped the children understand their father's preoccupation and made all my effort worthwhile. Finally, in the dedication of this volume I have tried to express my appreciation to two individuals whose confidence sustained me in this work as it has so often in the past.

J.C.C.

Contents

I

Back Country Survival

THE RETURN OF SPRING brought peace to New Orleans in 1815. Never had the change of seasons been more welcome. For over two years the city had dreaded attack; rumors flew that the British army intended to ravage the town, rape the women, free the slaves. "You've heard I suppose of New Orleans," the American defenders later sang:

> Tis famed for youth and beauty
> There're girls of every hue, it seems
> From Snowy White to Sooty.
>
> Now Pakenham had made his brags
> If that Day he was lucky
> He'd have those girls and cotton bags ...

When suddenly, in the stecly mists of a cold January morning came the miraculous deliverance:

> Jackson he was wide awake
> And was not scared of trifles
>
> For well he knew Kentucky boys
> With their death-dealing rifles.

Now, as the rifles fell silent, the smell of spring replaced the stench of death. At his headquarters in New Orleans, America's newest military hero took a brief leave from trifling civilian concerns to celebrate his forty-eighth birthday and to reflect on his stunning victory. Characteristically, his thoughts ran to tragedy, not triumph, as he recalled the painful period when his mother died. "Gentlemen, How I wish *she* could have lived to see this day," he told his aides. "There never was a woman like her."

In these seemingly innocent and reverent musings, Andrew Jackson tried once again to resolve his ambivalent feelings about the past. He had grown up in a chaotic environment, lacking the normal security of family, church, and community; these beginnings fostered an anger and insecurity that troubled him through life.

His parents, Elizabeth and Andrew Jackson, were raised in Ulster, Northern Ireland, at a time of economic and social upheaval. The beginnings of the Industrial Revolution upset the traditional patterns of tenant farming, forcing many families to seek their living in the growing woolen trades. Crop failures, rising rents, declining incomes—all contributed to the instability. Many Scotch-Irish farmers, finding adjustment to the new conditions impossible, heeded the calls of colonial agents who advertised the promise of America. Elizabeth Jackson's sisters joined the migration as did her brother-in-law Hugh, for whom the military offered escape. Finally, in 1765 the Jacksons and their two young sons followed their relatives to the New World.

The immigrant couple found themselves in a society nearly as disrupted as the one they had abandoned. They were among the last in the great wave of Ulster migration that had begun early in the eighteenth century. By the eve of the War for Independence, nearly 250,000 Scotch-Irish had made the difficult Atlantic crossing. Pouring into Pennsylvania, the newcomers bought whatever land they could find, sending already inflated prices soaring even higher. When the Jacksons debarked, they had little choice but to head South, along the great wagon road that connected Pennsylvania with the back country of the Carolinas. They were not alone. Along this route traveled thousands of immigrants who, like the Jacksons, hoped to begin life anew. Purchasing land from speculators or from other migrants who moved further south, the new arrivals tried to establish homesteads on the red piedmont soil.

Andrew Jackson chose a site along Twelve Mile Creek in a Catawba River valley known as the Waxhaws. He could not afford better land and so was separated from Elizabeth's relatives, who lived on more fertile tracts five miles away. In the Waxhaws the comfort of kinfolk was as precious as the soil itself.

Andrew Jackson and his wife settled in an isolated, frontier region with few governmental institutions and fragile communications with the outside world. The residents were still in a state of shock from the Cherokee War, which had devastated the back country five years earlier. During this bloody conflict, families moved constantly, fearing for life and property, often leaving their belongings to the mercy of the Indians and vagabonds. Lawlessness dominated the area. Settlers had no protection from Indian reprisals; they demanded that Carolina politicians bring order to the uplands, but to no avail. Eastern landowners, burdened by economic problems and concerned about possible slave revolts, showed little sympathy for the back country, where they saw few slaves or resources worth protecting.

Ethnic diversity further complicated the problems of the Carolina piedmont. Germans, Swiss, Scotch-Irish, and "native Virginians" vied for territorial supremacy. This intense competition gave rise to numerous disputes that the primitive court structure could not handle. Violence and bloodshed became accepted means of resolving conflict. Religion offered a potential source of social control, but as long as the various denominations contended for converts, its impact remained minimal. In fact, the chaotic conditions of back country churches greatly increased social instability. Empty pulpits, uncertain finances, primitive schools—all inhibited the growth of strong religious institutions. Confronted by these harsh realities, the various ethnic groups turned inward, looking for ways to combine with kinfolk and bring order. Clannishness promoted some beneficial social change but divided the back country into small, isolated ethnic enclaves.

Scotch-Irish settlers managed to bring some order to the Waxhaws. Despite its remoteness, this settlement was one of the most densely populated areas in the back country. During the 1760s a limited trade sprang up with Charleston, and this tended to reduce the isolation. Waxhaw residents built a substantial church, providing the essential disciplinary mechanisms to enforce a strict brand of Presbyterianism. When the itinerant Anglican minister Charles Woodmason visited the region, he found a large, thriving congregation and an even greater back country rarity—an educated minister. Woodmason noted, no doubt with a bit of satisfaction, that many covert Anglicans chafed under Presbyterian domination. This religious tension would remain an obstacle to Scotch-Irish efforts to build a unified community.

For the Jackson family, personal tragedy compounded the problems of frontier insecurity. Having survived the arduous ocean crossing and the long trek to Carolina, Elizabeth's husband died suddenly while working on the new homestead. His son would later claim that he "died like a hero in battle, fighting for his wife and babes; fighting an uphill battle against poverty and adversity as no one in our generation could comprehend." Perhaps local custom embellished this accident. More likely, Jackson sorely missed a father and needed to construct and believe in such a heroic death.

Already seven-months pregnant at the time of her husband's death, Elizabeth Jackson found it impossible to maintain the cabin at Twelve Mile Creek and went to live with her sister, Jane Crawford. There, on March 15, 1767, she gave birth to a son whom she named after her dead husband.

Despite the anguish and shock of displacement, life in the Crawford household was relatively comfortable. James Crawford owned a substantial tract of land, worked by a sizable number of slaves. He welcomed Elizabeth to the fold; she could take care of the domestic chores since his own wife was an invalid. Elizabeth took charge of a large household that now included eleven children. Andrew grew up amid constant bustle and had to cope with considerable confusion of adult roles: an uncle who could never be a true father, a crippled aunt unable to care for even her own children, and a mother who remained a house guest no matter how great her responsibilities.

Elizabeth Jackson dreamed that her son would become a minister. Religion meant a great deal to her, as it did to most Waxhaw settlers. Like the New England Puritans, Scotch-Irish Presbyterians practiced an active, outgoing faith. They hoped to stimulate conversion while creating a stable community. Fortunate to have a full-time minister, they planned to build their lives around the church and make it the source of both spiritual nourishment and social regimentation. Elizabeth Jackson's dream showed both her piety and her ambition. She wanted nothing less than that Andrew should become a community leader and through religious training achieve both the status and power associated with the ministerial profession. Subsequent events soon gave her great cause for concern.

Already one of the largest back country congregations, the Waxhaw Church soon became the most troubled. Disagreement arose over the sensitive matter of the minister's orthodoxy. Reverend Richardson shocked some of his parishioners by trying to introduce a new Psalm book; they clung tenaciously to the traditional Ulster version. Their suspicions aroused, church members began to examine other aspects of the minister's life. The good Reverend seemed to prosper too easily. His large plantation house and his regular literary gatherings prompted hushed complaints, especially among nonchurch members who already had reason to resent Presbyterian dominance. Not content with his ministrations at the Waxhaws, Reverend Richardson traveled widely throughout the back country, helping to found other churches. Such extended absences sparked additional criticism.

On the evening of July 21, 1771, the Waxhaw minister was found dead in his study, a bridle lashed around his neck. At first the church governors tried to hide the evidence of foul play, claiming that Reverend Richardson had died during devotion. Word of the bridle soon leaked out, and when the minister's bereaved widow promptly married a local plantation owner, rumor ran rampant. For a year debate raged. Finally, the congregation exhumed the minister's body and, in a highly emotional ritual, forced Richardson's widow to touch the decaying skull. When her hand did not bleed, tradition declared her innocent.

This macabre scene showed the intense social tensions in the Waxhaws. Among such a dispersed, rural population, the church provided a place to meet, to discuss common concerns, and to reach decisions that could be relayed to the countryside. Waxhaw pioneers saw the back country beset by vagrancy, illegitimacy, crime, violence, and barbarity. The church offered solutions, discipline, and a code of conduct. Church members took their responsibilities seriously, monitoring their own behavior, that of their neighbors, and even that of their minister. In such a setting, with so much at stake, even a minor theological dispute assumed major social significance.

Once the murder took place, the congregation had to eradicate the aura of scandal. They could not tolerate such a threat to the community. They had to find Richardson's widow guilty or conclusively establish her innocence; either result would clear his name and the reputation of the church. Only ancestral custom could sway the doubtful, and so the medieval graveside ceremony took place. Despite this dramatic ritual, the church temporarily lost its hold over the community. As a staunch church member, Elizabeth Jackson clung to the hope that order would return and that the ministry would regain its stature; her son Andrew might yet find it an honorable and powerful profession. At the very least she hoped religion would save this untamable youth, who fast was becoming a champion hell-raiser.

All accounts of Andrew Jackson's youth mention his wildness, yet few explain the cause, except to attribute it to the Scotch-Irish temperament and penchant for violent outdoor activity. High spirits were normal, especially in such an undisciplined environment, but the boy's behavior reached extremes. He entered everything with almost reckless abandon. He was the "most mischievous of youngsters thereabouts," recalled an old slave woman on the Crawford plantation. Perhaps he had to be, simply to gain attention in a large family in which he was the youngest. Notoriety he received, but little discipline. Doubtless his mother tried to control the excessive behavior, but her own circumstances made guidance difficult. Scotch-Irish society assigned females household chores and field work, reserving to males the important decisions affecting the economic destiny of their offspring. Even after her sister died, Elizabeth was not formal mistress of her own house. Andrew no doubt recognized his mother's subservient role and found it unworthy of imitation.

Nor could Mr. Humphries, the local schoolmaster, transform the young hellion. He taught Andrew to read and write, but little more. Throughout a long, famous career, Jackson misused the English language: his grammar was uncertain, his sentences incomplete, and his spelling atrocious. Considering his lack of formal education and the incoherent prose of some of his contemporaries, he did not fare too badly. He expressed himself directly, at times too directly. He mangled words but seldom minced them. As president he had the good sense to submit most of his public writing to the criticism of friends, who improved the style but seldom altered the content. The Carolina back country did not provide leisure or incentive for a contemplative life, and Jackson never developed a love of books or of abstract ideas. He had a practical mind and when young seemed totally preoccupied with finding his place among his peers.

The standing that he could not achieve within the Crawford household, Andrew won outdoors in endless hours of racing, fighting, and frolic. He was an excellent horseman, but this was not enough. He had to master the "sport of kings"; to his dying day, Jackson showed an almost compulsive interest in horse racing. As president, he kept race horses in the White House stables.

Although fond of mimicry and crude levity, Andrew was not a particularly happy youngster. He was often cantankerous and extremely defensive. In part this sensitivity had physical origins. He was never robust and early in life suffered a serious skin disease known as the "big itch," which no doubt added to his irascibility. Until he reached adulthood, he tended to slobber, a very embarrassing impediment about which he would tolerate no comment. He was extremely sensitive to criticism in general and would try to punish anyone who ridiculed him, no matter how slight the offense. He had an ugly temper, was full of anger that he could not control, and lost no opportunity to vent his aggressions. He thrived on conflict, yet even when victorious never allowed himself to feel triumphant. He continually needed to prove himself. In short, he was a violent and unpredictable youngster—a most difficult but lively companion.

Time might have smoothed the rough edges, but just as he reached adolescence, Andrew was plunged into the horror and confusion of war. It was not at all what he had expected. He had long dreamed of soldiering; much of his recreation took the form of mock military exercise. In these games he had become a leader and hoped that if war came, he would be old enough to fight. He spent long evening hours at the fireside, listening to his mother recount the exploits of Ulster heroes and thrilling to the stories of his Uncle Hugh's military adventures.

The War for Independence was not like the war of legend and fancy. It directly touched the Waxhaws, filling the church with wounded and dying soldiers, some not much older than Andrew himself. He helped his mother minister to these victims, and the sight of so much suffering must have come as a shock. Then his relatives began returning, scarred from battle. Some never returned. His brother Hugh died from exposure following a vicious summer fight at Stono Ferry. The British advanced on the Waxhaws and the Crawfords fled, seeking refuge where they could. Not since the Cherokee War nearly two decades earlier had there been so much confusion. Loyalists rallied to the side of the invading troops, while families like the Jacksons clung tenaciously to the cause of the Continental Congress. Neighbor fought neighbor; violence and murder swept the area in the wake of battle. Spies were everywhere.

In the spring of 1781, acting on information supplied by a Waxhaw loyalist, British troops captured a number of young militiamen, including Andrew and his brother Robert. Now a helpless witness to the looting and pillage, Andrew was further humiliated when a British officer demanded that he play the role of servant. When Andrew refused to clean the officer's boots, he narrowly missed being decapitated. The sword blow left a deep scar, as did the other events of his captivity.

Andrew had no idea how long he would be imprisoned or what his ultimate fate might be. Confined to a second-floor room of the district jail at Camden, South Carolina, he received no medical attention and little food. Smallpox broke out shortly after he arrived, threatening to devastate the prisoners. He escaped after a few weeks, thanks to the boldness of his mother who successfully pleaded with British commanders to release her sons in exchange for English soldiers. By the time he left Camden, Andrew was seriously ill with a raging fever. He walked behind his brother Robert, who was so sick from the smallpox that he had to be tied on a horse. Within two days of their liberation Robert was dead. Andrew took little notice as he was delirious with fever. His mother nursed him as best she could, but she had many obligations. Two of Andrew's cousins lay sick on a British prison ship off Charleston. Having cared for so many strangers, she could not refuse the appeal of relatives. She left her feverish son in bed and set off for Charleston. She never returned. Fever took her life as it took so many during the war. The once proud soldier boy was now an orphan.

The tragedy left deep scars on Andrew Jackson's personality. The loss of his brother Hugh had first caused him to confront the possibility of death at an early age. His mother and remaining brother had calmed the fears. Now they too were suddenly gone, leaving him no protection against the awful finality of death. Fever shielded him for a time, but it could not stay the inevitable agony of introspection. No record of his exact thoughts exists, but his subsequent behavior suggests that he was consumed with anger and guilt. Perhaps he felt responsible for his mother's death, thinking that she had contracted his sickness. He had every reason to resent her decision to comfort two cousins while a son lay suffering. If so, her death must have made him feel doubly guilty for having harbored such thoughts. Certainly he wondered why he had been spared while his whole family had perished. Worse still, he had no way to resolve these feelings. Fate denied his mother a public funeral, thus preventing the comfort of ceremonial mourning. Her body never returned to the Waxhaws but lay in an unmarked grave in Charleston.

The passage of time brought little relief. After his mother's death, Jackson led an aimless existence. The bleak prospects brightened briefly when he learned that his grandfather had left him nearly four hundred pounds. He set off for Charleston to claim his inheritance. In 1783, such a sum represented a substantial stake in life; he might have used the money to purchase land, especially since he would inherit none from the Crawfords. Instead, he seized life with a vengeance, squandering his legacy on momentary pleasures. A fine horse, a gold watch, a brace of pistols, a new suit of clothes—these were more to his liking. He could pretend to be a gentleman and forget the bleak back country. The money soon evaporated and he went into debt. Only a stroke of luck prevented total disaster. Betting his horse in a dice game, Jackson recouped enough to satisfy his creditors.

Wild oats? Perhaps, but these escapades resemble the delinquent behavior often observed in adolescents who have confronted similar traumatic proof of their own mortality. In such situations, lavish expenditures of money and emotions represent a kind of mourning. That Jackson had his fling at the scene of his mother's demise underscores this point, for he had come to Charleston in search of his birthright but also to reckon with death. The reckoning never occurred. He tried in vain to locate his mother's grave. Denied even this consolation, he indulged himself in every way, rebelling against all the old maternal preachments. Excitement, glamor, fellowship, escape—everything but relief. When the money ran out, when the companions turned away, the guilt and the anguish remained.

For the rest of his life, Andrew Jackson tried to resolve the awful anxieties of this adolescent trauma. Like many other survivors he made martyrs of the dead. "She was as gentle as a dove and as brave as a lioness," he said of his mother three decades later. By idealizing his childhood and honoring his mother's errand of mercy, Jackson attempted to profit from his sorrow. "The memory of my mother and her teachings were after all the only capital I had to start my life with." He convinced himself that he had been spared to create the kind of life that she had always cherished: a life of honor, a life of courage, a life of order. In such a full life there would be no room for fear of death.

In his quest for such a life, Jackson encountered numerous emotional obstacles. Idealize through he might, his childhood had been far from ideal. He could honor his mother's bravery, but not without awakening fears of rejection. At that critical juncture in his adolescence, his cousins' well-being had apparently taken precedence over his own. Nor could he contemplate the meaning of his mother's sacrifice without recalling the *fact* of her demise. "When the tidings of her death reached me I at first could not believe it, when I finally realized the truth, I felt utterly alone." Alone and angry. Andrew Jackson could not express his anger directly for in doing so he would undermine the image of his mother as martyr, an image vital to his own peace of mind. "If ever you have to vindicate your feelings or defend your honor, do it calmly," she had counseled shortly before leaving for Charleston. "If angry at first, wait till your anger cools before you proceed." Jackson rarely let his wrath cool, but he justified it to himself by projecting his own unacceptable emotions outward onto someone, something. There were always suitable scapegoats: the Indians, the British, the Bank. Believing himself under attack, Jackson felt exonerated for striking back. The battle joined, he could then renew his mission, triumph over the terrible fears that haunted him, and thereby reassert his right to survive.

Financially and emotionally spent, Jackson left Charleston in 1783 and returned to the Waxhaws. He boarded with relatives, but the situation soon became intolerable. They expected him to accept responsibility, to merge his interests with those of the family. Jackson resisted; he had sacrificed enough. Thereafter he moved from one house to another, never feeling at home. His relatives strongly disapproved of his wild behavior and predicted that he would eventually disgrace the family name. When he finally decided to leave the Waxhaws for North Carolina, they felt relieved. He carried away bitter memories. "Homeless and friendless" were words Jackson later used to describe this period of his life.

The conclusion of the war and the adoption of a peace created new opportunities for America's aspiring young. The Treaty of Paris removed the twenty-year-old British restrictions on colonial expansion. Hunger for land, so long held in check, threatened to start a stampede across the mountains. Wherever there was land to claim, there was a need for legal talent, a commodity in short supply in the 1780s. Lawyers had played a prominent role in the coming of the revolution, but those who supported the crown found it difficult to resume practice in the postwar period. Opportunity beckoned, offering handsome rewards. Andrew Jackson decided to become a lawyer.

In eighteenth-century America, legal training was quite personal in nature. Back country society did not insist on formal legal education but did require students to read with a recognized jurist before requesting permission to practice. Never one who lacked ambition or daring, Jackson sought out the best Carolina back country lawyer, Waightstill Avery of Morgantown, North Carolina, and pleaded to become his apprentice. Avery refused and the aspiring advocate retraced his steps to the old colonial village of Salisbury, where he gained admission to the office of Spruce McCay. "Office" is hardly the correct term for a sixteen-by-fifteen-foot room where Jackson and two friends studied the legal trade. Fortunately, the cramped working space did not double as a boarding house, and they were able to take up lodgings at a nearby tavern.

Andrew Jackson soon became the talk of Salisbury. "Why when he was here, he was such a rake that my husband would not let him in the house," a village matron later recalled. "It is true," she continued, "he might have taken him out to the stables to weigh horses for a race, and might drink a glass of whiskey with him there." It was a wonder that Jackson found time to learn the law at all. He indulged himself in every way. His narrow escape from Charleston taught him little about managing money. He ran up tavern bills and then looked for ways to run away from them. At times the debts came from bizarre and violent events. In one legendary escapade, Jackson and his companions crashed into a banquet, tearing apart the room and destroying all the furniture. By all accounts he was "the most roaring, rollicking, game-cocking fellow, that ever lived in Salisbury" and served as "head of the rowdies hereabouts." "I was but a raw lad then," Jackson remarked later, "but I did my best."

At times, his best included polite, even charming behavior. Salisbury's young ladies had heard all the rumors about fighting, gambling, and a mulatto mistress. "We all knew that he was wild . . . and was by no means a christian man." Still, "his ways and manners were most captivating." Standing over six feet tall, the young law student was remarkably slender. Although agile and athletic, he was never considered handsome. He had sharp, angular features and a pale, freckled complexion. His "abundant suit of red hair" flew out in all directions, and he tried to tame it with liberal doses of "bear's oil." In conversation he was candid and direct. One young admirer recalled his "steel blue" eyes that "never left me for an instant. . . . This and the gentle manner made you forget the plainness of his features." Jackson could be gentle; when in control of his emotions he spoke slowly and with conviction. Yet he was always at war with himself, and when excited, he forgot polite conventions and poured forth a torrent of words in a high-pitched voice "with a very marked North-Irish accent."

Jackson may have wooed and won the hearts of the young ladies, but he angered their parents who "thought he would get himself killed before he was many years older." Jackson seemed entirely callous to the feelings of others. As an organizer of the annual Christmas ball, he sent invitations to the town prostitutes, merely as "a piece of fun," he claimed. The idea may have been amusing; their appearance was not. Nor was Spruce McCay terribly amused by his apprentice's notoriety. While another of Jackson's classmates, John McNairy, completed his training and gained admission to the bar, Jackson dawdled along. During the year that had passed since he took up study he had shown more interest in brawling than in Blackstone.

McCay enjoyed considerable stature in Salisbury and found Jackson's behavior embarrassing. Apparently the two argued, and Jackson left to read with another prominent attorney, John Stokes. As a revolutionary war hero and former convalescent

in the Waxhaws, Stokes thought more kindly of his new protégé. He drank heavily himself and made little attempt to curb
Jackson's excesses. In six months, Stokes covered enough law
so that Jackson could join the itinerant court at Wades-
borough, North Carolina. There on September 20, 1787, Jackson officially gained permission to practice.

Permission was one thing, practice another. The new advocate had little to advocate. No clients rushed to his office, for
he had no office. He lacked even an official residence. Ostra-
cized in the Waxhaws, unwelcome in Salisbury, he could not
compete with prominent eastern attorneys whose assets included established wealth and family prestige. For a time he
drifted, until, unable to find clients, he stopped in Martinsville,
North Carolina, where he tended store and tried to impress
the town fathers. They cared little for his legal talents for they
had lawyers of their own, but they made use of his knowledge
of gentlemanly sports. At a celebration of the Battle of Guil-
ford Court House, Jackson helped organize a cock fight and a
horse race. While in Martinsville, he renewed acquaintances
with his classmate John McNairy, whose family enjoyed considerable prominence and included in its circle of friends the
governor of North Carolina. This influence soon paid divi-
dends.

In late December 1787, the North Carolina legislature
moved to establish judicial control over the western reaches of
the state. Stretching from the Appalachian mountains to the
Mississippi River, this vast hinterland had already attracted a
sizable number of settlers. Legislators had to provide some
elementary mechanisms for resolving the inevitable disputes
that settlement entailed. The legislature could not act on such
distant conflicts itself, and, for the sake of efficiency, it created
a western district superior court. Young John McNairy agreed
to serve on the bench and in turn named Jackson as a public
prosecutor.

Although he now had a job, Jackson was hardly the envy of
the legal profession. Few established lawyers were willing to

give up the security of a settled practice for the uncertainty of the frontier, no matter how attractive the financial rewards. Jackson saw things differently. Without family, with few friends, he was free to go where he pleased. Granted the West had none of the charm of Charleston, or even the relative security of the Waxhaws, but it did offer him the opportunity to capitalize on a meagre training and to fulfill his insatiable desire to become a gentleman. In the company of John McNairy and several other members of the new court, Jackson set out for the Cumberland River in the spring of 1788. They crossed the mountains and stopped to practice law for a time in Jonesborough. Jackson wasted little time in trying to establish his gentlemanly credentials: in his short stay in Jonesborough, he bought a slave and fought a duel.

Andrew Jackson grew up in a slaveholding society that regarded blacks as chattels. Slaves provided labor and formed a status barrier, beneath which whites believed they could never sink. Throughout his life, Jackson supported the peculiar institution. Although he expressed some concern over the proper treatment of slaves, he never questioned the legitimacy of slavery. Nor did he philosophize about the position of blacks in American society. Clearly he believed them inferior, although he manifested some fondness for his house servants. His correspondence on the subject concerns plantation operations and reveals none of the anguish and guilt of another, more introspective, slaveholding president, Thomas Jefferson. In 1788 Jackson had no property and very few resources, yet somehow he found $300 to purchase a "negro woman named Nancy, about eighteen or twenty years of age" from one Micajah Crews. Jackson had little use for the domestic services of a slave; the purchase conferred a measure of status.

Before departing for the Cumberland, Jackson again demonstrated his peculiar propensity for attracting controversy. Among those appearing before the Jonesborough Court was Waightstill Avery, the prominent attorney who had refused to accept Jackson as an apprentice. An extremely skillful advocate, Avery delighted courthouse audiences with his sharp wit and sarcasm. Jackson chanced to be his opponent one day and felt the full brunt of Avery's attack. The young lawyer took offense at Avery's tactics, interpreting them as personal ridicule. Tearing a page from his law book, Jackson scribbled a note and hurled it at his surprised adversary. A formal challenge followed. "You have insulted me in the presence of a court and a large audience," Jackson claimed. "I therefore call upon you to give me satisfaction for the same." Avery tried to dissuade his young colleague from such precipitous action, but Jackson was intent on revenge. The two met outside of town, went through the correct formalities, exchanged harmless shots, and then walked off the field of honor, fully reconciled. This was the first of many duels in which Jackson was either a participant or a second.

The duel and the code of honor underlying it reveal a great deal about Andrew Jackson and the society of his times. On one level, the duel reflected the hazards of a free people's belief in the inalienable right to bear arms. Possession of arms implied the need to learn martial skills and in turn led to demonstrations of prowess. Although most people could master the rudiments of musketry, few learned the intricate details of the duel. The duel was a convention that performed an important function in Southern society, especially in western areas where social structure was not yet rigidly stratified. The duel helped preserve honor, that indefinable concept that separated the gentleman from the savage. Loss of honor meant loss of respect, loss of reputation, and eventually loss of standing in the community. No gentleman could refuse a challenge without risking such consequences. In a society with few law enforcement agencies, the code of honor provided a mechanism for resolving internal conflicts and for establishing and maintaining credentials necessary for acceptance into the aristocracy.

In this sense the Avery duel is enormously significant. When Jackson reached Jonesborough, he had neither renown nor prestige. Within two months he laid claim to both. He had purchased a slave, thereby identifying himself, however modestly, with the planter class, and he had forced a recognized gentleman to give him satisfaction. He had therefore established his honor, which in view of his precarious finances was a precious commodity. He had proclaimed to all Jonesborough that, despite his violent temper, he was an honorable man, a gentleman.

Jackson took satisfaction from his encounter with Avery. He had silenced a slanderer, a human species he considered "worse than a murderer." "The murderer only takes the life of the parent and leaves his character as a goodly heritage to his children, whilst the slanderer takes away his good reputation and leaves him a living monument to his children's disgrace." Slander would always plague Andrew Jackson's troubled world; he would have to be eternally vigilant. Death had spared him, but only for a purpose: to build the "goodly heritage" that could justify his mother's sacrifice and his own survival. This first, successful appeal to the code confirmed Jackson's sense of mission and convinced him that prompt retaliation alone would curb corruption and silence slander.

For the moment the tongues were still. He had arrived and having arrived was ready to move further west.

II

Risks and Rewards

IMPETUOSITY, BOASTFULNESS, recklessness, daring —such traits were out of place in genteel tidewater society; in middle Tennessee, they stood a man in good stead. Barely a decade old, the Cumberland colony of Nashville was just beginning to win a harrowing struggle for survival. Military proficiency still counted most heavily in the emerging social structure, but by 1788, when Andrew Jackson arrived, the colonists had a desperate need of legal services and political organization. Having seized the land, they had to develop the legal mechanisms and social institutions to hold it.

Nashville's rough dwellings housed great ambitions. The pioneers who migrated to the Cumberland region during the waning years of the War for Independence came not as individuals, but as members of a paternalistic enterprise, led and financed by men of wealth and determination. The father of middle Tennessee, soft-spoken James Robertson, had long been interested in western colonization. A skilled treaty negotiator, he used his position as Indian agent to appraise the choice land west of the mountains. Robertson associated with wealthy speculators, was adept at managing military affairs, had previous experience in frontier settlement, and earned the respect of colonists. His partner in the Cumberland expedition was fifty-four-year-old John Donelson, a large and fleshy patriarch whose family figured prominently in Tennessee history for the next century. Donelson had little experience with the

Indians, but he brought other assets to the expeditions. His family owned iron mines in Virginia; with these resources he could purchase land. As a surveyor and militia colonel, he had the connections and technical skills to claim a large share of Tennessee's future.

Together with other prominent speculators, these frontier entrepreneurs acquired huge tracts of forest, some for their own use, the rest to sell at a profit. Although eager to extinguish its revolutionary war debts by the sale of western land, North Carolina tried to brake this headlong rush by imposing a 5,000-acre limit on individual claims, but the speculators circumvented these restrictions with ease. Often they formed land companies to increase both their capital and the efficiency of their efforts. They succeeded because they were resourceful and self-reliant. Willing to travel and live in the wilderness, they located choice sites before they appeared on a surveyor's map or land register. In fact, the speculators monopolized most of the essential mechanisms for land acquisition, acting as surveyors and sellers, pioneers and patrons. Subsequent settlers had little choice but to purchase homesteads from these wealthy magnates. If Indian claims intruded, men like James Robertson could persuade the tribes to make cessions. Furthermore, the large speculating families of John Donelson, William Blount, Richard Henderson, and William Polk had sufficient political power to obtain special favors from the North Carolina legislature. They also held offices that controlled back country life and were useful on the frontier. The Cumberland no less than the Carolinas needed justices of the peace, sheriffs, and county courts. Through these institutions, the wealthy established control over the new land. By 1787 only one out of every eight adult white males in the Cumberland basin owned land.

The elite did not maintain control without challenge. According to one estimate, from 1780 to 1794 Indians killed an average of one person every ten days within a five-mile radius of Nashville. Thirty settlers died in 1788, the year Jackson reached the settlement. Relations between the whites and the Indians reflected over a century of bloodshed. Tennessee's pioneers regarded the Indians as savages who forfeited all property rights because of their barbarity and nomadic life style. To till the land, tame the forest, triumph over the environment—these were the goals of colonization and civilization. Whites might learn to survive in the forest, but they would never respect their Indian tutors. So long as their insatiable desire for land provoked resistance, white colonists insisted on retaliation. They had little faith in a federal policy of accommodation. All adult males in the Cumberland basin were required to bear arms, and the militia soon became a major agency for community action. But the forts, the musters, the drills, even the successful expeditions against the Indians never eased the terrible fear that pervaded early Cumberland society. The Cumberland suffered both ambition and anxiety in excess.

Because he had similar hopes and fears, Andrew Jackson readily adapted to his new surroundings. He was by no means a pioneer, but he did share the aspirations of the original settlers. As one of his closest associates later recalled, Jackson and his traveling companions in 1788 were "all lawyers seeking their fortunes." Like many of his new Nashville acquaintances, Jackson never enjoyed good fortune in the east. He lacked the family connections, property, and political standing to enter the lists of the tidewater aristocracy. Yet aristocrat he wanted to be—if not in Charleston, then certainly on the Cumberland. In the unsettled society of the new colony, Jackson expected his legal skills to compensate for his lack of family connections and education.

The young advocate easily accommodated his own prejudices to those of his new neighbors. Cumberland residents suspected that eastern politicians were seeking to limit the new Republic to the eastern seaboard, leaving the Cumberland to the mercy of the Indians. At the same time, Nashville's founders struggled to replicate tidewater society, complete with races, duels, and slave quarters.

Jackson shared other attitudes as well. Although he had never fought against the Indians nor lost any member of his immediate family in an Indian attack, he held pronounced views on red-white relations. Ancestral tales of massacres near the Waxhaws extolled white bravery and martial skill and left him the belief that he would one day have to test himself in combat against the ancient, legendary enemy. Jackson's early correspondence occasionally mentioned Indian affairs, and always in the most revealing terms. Like most westerners, Jackson considered the Indian a savage, a term that connoted not only the absence of civilized behavior but a total lack of redeeming religious belief or common morality. He could not understand politicians who advocated peaceful disposition of Indian problems. "Some say humanity dictates it," Jackson wrote angrily in 1794, demanding "an equal share of humanity to our own citizens" and punishment for "the Barbarians for murdering the innocent." On the subject of treaties, Jackson was equally exercised. "I fear that our peace talks are only delusions. . . . Treaties answer no other purpose than opening an Easy door for the Indians to pass through to Butcher our citizens." He warned that if the Cumberland could not obtain adequate support from the east, it might "seek protection from some other source."

Although couched in the familiar rhetoric of frontier vengeance, Jackson's remarks revealed a very personal aversion to Indian savagery. Indians represented disorder, a threat to white family solidarity and community stability, the lack of which contributed to Jackson's own wildness, anger, and insecurity. In reacting to the shock of his mother's death, he tried to disown his troubled childhood, replacing it with aspirations for an orderly life. He could not begin to build such a life so long as the very land that promised security was threatened. For what status would Jackson achieve with the "frontier Discouraged and breaking," with people "leaving the territory and moving to Kentucky"? "This country is declining fast," he complained. Rather than admit that his own ambition and that of his contemporaries led directly to such instability, Jackson lashed out at the Indians. They were doubly evil, reminding him of a past he was trying to forget and threatening a future he was trying to achieve. The Indian was a fit target for wrath.

Andrew Jackson needed to release his ire, for status exacted its price. The wild back country youth had to bend to social conventions; like the hickory, he never bent easily. Anger and frustration always ran perilously close to the surface of his behavior, the more so because he continually encountered reminders of his troubled past. When such memories welled up, he lashed out. "Barbarian," "savage," and "butcher" were words of hatred, but they were socially acceptable. Jackson feared and hated the Indian, but in a sense he needed him, too, just as he would need other enemies throughout his career.

A lawyer who would legitimize the claims of speculators, speak out boldly in favor of military retaliation, and was apparently willing to defend his views by force if necessary was useful in the Cumberland. Within three months after his arrival, Jackson found himself involved in the Spanish Conspiracy, a minor but significant episode in frontier diplomacy. The plot involved relations between the United States and Spain. In 1784 Spain decided to strengthen its control over the Gulf Coast by closing the Mississippi River to American trade. Although the closure posed no immediate commercial threat to the infant Cumberland settlement, it would definitely hamper future development. When the Creek Indians began a series of raids on the southern frontier in 1786, the colonists perceived a vast Spanish plot to drive them from the land. Their fears increased when Congress refused to challenge the Spanish decision and when North Carolina failed to finance military expeditions against the Creeks. Convinced that they were being sacrificed to Northern interests, Southern colonists decided to mount a diplomatic offensive of their own. They began negotiations with Spanish representatives, offering to break off from the United States and recognize Spanish sovereignty in return for an end to the commercial and military pressure. Tennesseans hoped that their ploy would force North Carolina to cede its western lands to Congress, thus bringing the Cumberland under federal control. Eventually this plan succeeded. Although he played a minor role in this "conspiracy," Jackson had obviously won the respect of the elite, who felt secure in using him as an intermediary.

Jackson further earned this trust by his administration of the law, a scarce commodity in Nashville. In the original plans for Nashville, the town fathers specified construction of a district jail, a set of stocks, and a courthouse eighteen feet square. They built the stocks and the jail, but justice had to await more prosperous times. Lack of adequate housing proved no impediment to the growth of the frontier court; Jackson and his fellow attorneys never wanted for work. A decade of disputed land titles, assault cases, and bad debts flooded the docket. In a given year, Jackson handled as much as one-half of this volume. Such monopoly was not uncommon in frontier jurisprudence, for the court was an informal, independent organization that contracted with the public to do its business. The judge presided, and in a sense lawyers were his attendants more than they were public servants. Jackson may have taken pleasure in belonging to such a thriving institution, but he soon discovered that a busy lawyer did not always prosper. Legal fees came in strange forms: specie, produce, horseflesh. Some never came. The judge alone had a guaranteed income, and soon after his admission to the Nashville bar in 1789, Jackson aspired to the bench.

Of those needing the court's assistance, Nashville's merchants clamored the loudest. They complained of being victimized by "adventurers from different sections of the country" who refused to honor their debts. As solicitor, Jackson reacted promptly to these pleas. In his first month of practice, he served over seventy writs on delinquent debtors. Those judged delinquent resented such efficient application of the law and tried to force the solicitor to leave. Without land or funds, they could hardly deter a man who was rapidly finding his calling. Within a year after his arrival in Nashville, Jackson won appointment as attorney general, a position that brought political as well as financial rewards.

Family connections also figured prominently in Jackson's successful quest for social status. Perhaps by accident, probably by design, Jackson took up lodgings with the Donelson clan, one of the most powerful families in middle Tennessee. Indians killed John Donelson in 1785, but his survivors had come too far to turn back. His widow built a large blockhouse near Neely's Bend, northeast of Nashville. Following French and Spanish custom, she took in young bachelors who boarded in the crude outbuildings and helped protect against Indian attacks. Jackson lived in "the cabin room, and slept in the same bed" with John Overton, a talented young attorney, whose knowledge of land law made him indispensable to wealthy speculators. Politics makes strange bedfellows, but in this instance the reverse was true. To his dying day, John Overton devoted a major portion of his time to the advancement of Jackson's politicial and commercial career. And when his friend was elected president, Overton burned much of their correspondence, leaving the exact nature of their relationship to the guesswork of biographers.

It requires little speculation to explain the Donelson clan's success. Stockley Donelson learned his father's skills and became a land surveyor. After locating choice property, he bought it and became the "largest land holder in East Tennessee." His brothers proved equally apt; buying up tracts in the central basin, they soon preempted the choicest Cumberland River locations. The family prospered and expanded but remained inbred. Suspicion of outsiders diminished in time; the intense pride and growing pretension did not. Though residing in log cabins, the Donelsons sent to New Orleans for furniture, bought slaves in Virginia, educated their children in private schools, and even designed a coat of arms. The familial network served as both a channel of culture and an avenue of advancement.

Barely a path in 1788, the way was clearly marked and Andrew Jackson read the signs with ease. This was not solely a journey of expediency. Jackson needed family ties; he had been wandering long enough. In the widow Donelson he saw a woman, much like his mother, who struggled to manage a large family. He also found himself attracted to her daughter Rachel, who unfortunately belonged to another man.

Most accounts of the fabled romance between Andrew Jackson and Rachel Donelson tell an incredibly intricate story of how Jackson came to the defense of the Donelson household; fell in love with raven-haired Rachel; threatened to cut the ears off her husband, Lewis Robards; dashed to Kentucky to rescue Rachel from her spouse's jealous rage; escorted her through hostile Indian country to Mississippi; reluctantly returned to law practice in Nashville; learned that Robards had sued for divorce; raced back to Mississippi and married Rachel; brought her in triumph to Tennessee; discovered to his horror that the divorce had not been final; suffered the indignity of a second ceremony; and then for over three decades stood ready to kill anyone with the effrontery to suggest that this courtship was in the least bit extraordinary.

Andrew Jackson's marriage became a frontier scandal, but it was a shrewd compact, designed to save the Donelson family name and advance the young lawyer's personal fortunes. The plan succeeded, but at a terrible cost. No matter how substantial the structure, or how cheerful the company, Jackson's house was continually troubled. The insecurity, suspicion, and doubt he had known as an adolescent, now magnified by his marriage and by Rachel's own anxiety, would disturb him throughout his adult life.

When Jackson came to board with the Donelsons, the rift between Rachel and her husband threatened to erupt into a

major scandal. Although frontier communu.
the formalities of the marriage ceremony, they s.
fended the sanctity of the family and abhorred divorce,
offended the natural order and upset social stability. Furthermore, it required costly and time-consuming investigation by
the state legislature. Naturally the Donelson family preferred
not to have its troubles opened to such official scrutiny. They
attempted on several occasions to reunite the estranged couple, but Robards's insane jealousy and Rachel's frequent flirtations made reconciliation difficult.

The Donelsons hoped that their new boarder could help
resolve this dilemma. They trusted Jackson, as they had previously trusted John Overton, to serve as intermediary between
the warring families. A man of law and a gentleman, Jackson
might be able to convince Robards that his suspicions were
groundless. When Jackson's love for Rachel made such neutrality impossible and led to open quarrels with Robards, the
Donelsons very likely presumed that he would resolve the
problem in an honorable way. In fact, Jackson challenged Robards to a duel, but the distraught husband refused. Although
a duel would have created its own scandal, it certainly would
have been quicker than a divorce. Had Jackson lost, then Robards would no longer have had grounds for suspicion. Soon
after this challenge failed, the Donelsons found themselves at
the mercy of public opinion and the law. No matter what the
grounds, divorce would dishonor the family name, for Rachel
would be cited for cause. As a divorced woman, she would live
in disgrace, a constant reminder of the breakdown in family
obligations. No doubt these thoughts weighed heavily on her
mind and drove her to seek refuge in Mississippi.

In the summer of 1791, news reached Nashville that Lewis
Robards had obtained a divorce from the Virginia legislature.
As a lawyer, Jackson should have known that legislatures rarely
granted divorces outright, usually investigating the charges
and, if substantiated, enabling the husband to sue in court.
Jackson probably knew these facts. Yet delay might permit

Robards to seek another reconciliation, thereby thwarting Jackson's efforts to marry Rachel and enter the Donelson family. If Robards did persist in the divorce, the attendant investigation and scandal might wreck Jackson's romance. Better to seize the moment, to pose as the defender of the Donelson family, to marry Rachel. Then, though the public might criticize his previous behavior, they would have no cause to doubt the honor of his intentions. Such headstrong actions involved tremendous risks. More than his own happiness and reputation hung in the balance. Yet Jackson had survived risks before. Spurred by ambition, goaded by a strong sense of his own rectitude, he rushed to the widow Donelson for her permission. "Mr. Jackson," the matriarch asked, "would you sacrifice your life to save my poor child's good name?" To which the calculating young solicitor replied: "Ten thousand lives, madam, if I had them."

Sacrifice there would be, but mostly on Rachel's part. Her youthful exuberance soon gave way to mounting anxieties. First came the news in December 1793 that Robards had only recently obtained a divorce. The Jacksons reluctantly agreed to recite their vows again. Although now official, the second ceremony caused Rachel untold anguish. She became deeply religious; her awkward, halting letters abounded with Biblical allusions. She sought comfort in the company of clergymen and later in life convinced her husband to become an active churchgoer. Yet no devotion, no prayer could purge her mind of the awful shame. She had no children and undoubtedly took this as a sign of divine retribution. Jackson tried to comfort as best he knew how, even convincing Rachel's cousin to let them adopt one of their twin boys. Jackson might have helped more by staying home, but ambition took him far away.

Andrew Jackson wanted to be a judge; to become a judge he first had to become a politician. His friendships and new family connections came to the attention of William Blount, the first governor of the new Southwest Territory. A powerful speculator and a shrewd politician, Blount rewarded those who had joined his successful campaign to have Congress legalize the great land grabs of the 1780s. James Robertson, brigadier general of the militia; Daniel Smith, secretary and surveyor of the territory; John McNairy, territorial judge—the list continues and includes the landed elite. Thanks to Blount's patronage, Jackson won reappointment as attorney general and then added another plum—judge advocate of the Davidson county militia. Though not powerful, the post had enormous potential. With every able-bodied male required to serve, the militia constituted the most extensive institution in the newly settled territory. The fear of Indian uprisings kept military matters constantly in the minds of the people. To the frightened colonists, the militia official, no less than an officer of the law, promised protection against the forces of disorder.

Armed with his legal training, his military title, and the governor's blessing, Jackson waged his campaign for property and standing. In 1796 he served as a member of the five-man Davidson county delegation to the constitutional convention in Knoxville. Having determined that the territory had more than the required 60,000 inhabitants, the Blount forces pushed for statehood. Jackson took little part in the Knoxville proceedings—unless we are to believe the legend that he suggested Tennessee as a name for the state. Tennessee it was— a peculiar piece of frontier perversity since the word is derived from the name of a Cherokee chieftain.

In 1796 Jackson's political chieftain, William Blount, was being directly challenged by east Tennessee's John Sevier (alias Nolichucky Jack). While Blount speculated and manipulated behind the scenes, Sevier strutted about center stage, parading his daring before an appreciative audience. The tall, handsome militia hero had an incredible string of victories including a revolutionary triumph at King's Mountain and a grizzly massacre of the Cherokees in 1794. In this so-called Nick-a-Jack expedition, Sevier's invaders, led by General James Robertson, swept into Cherokee towns, destroying log houses, burning grain fields, killing livestock, and razing fruit orchards. Sevier reaped immediate benefit from this awful harvest. When Tennessee held its first state elections in 1796, he captured the governor's chair. Temporarily stripped of state patronage, Blount shifted attention to the new federal offices, graciously accepting the legislature's offer to become a United States senator. He then cast about for a loyal candidate to stand election for Tennessee's lone seat in the House of Representatives. His choice, and ultimately that of the people, was the young judge advocate of the Davidson County Militia.

During the next two years, Andrew Jackson served as both congressman and senator. Neither office held much attraction for him, nor did he distinguish himself in federal politics. Being the hand-picked representative of William Blount carried great prestige in Tennessee, but not in Philadelphia, where the name Blount (pronounced "blunt") became synonymous with conspiracy and intrigue. In 1797 the Senate expelled William Blount, claiming that he was planning a filibustering expedition against Florida. Tennessee legislators reacted angrily to the expulsion and promptly installed Blount as president of the state senate. Then for good measure, they appointed Andrew Jackson to succeed Blount in the United States Senate.

Because his constituency was so provincial and because Tennessee itself was often at odds with the administration, Andrew Jackson felt extremely uncomfortable in national politics. Like his fellow Tennesseans, he distrusted the central government, believing that such measures as Jay's Treaty showed a callous disregard for Western interests, especially the crucial right to sail the Mississippi. Jackson rarely rose to register his dismay. Instead he contented himself with symbolic protests. At the end of his first session in Congress, Jackson refused to join in a vote of tribute for outgoing President George Washington. When Jackson did rise it was to speak on behalf of frontier preparedness. As congressman, he introduced a bill to reimburse Tennessee's expenses on the

Nick-a-Jack expedition of 1794. The young congressman was more angry than eloquent. He spoke of the savage barbarity of the frontier, of the tomahawk and the scalping knife. Having heard such blusterings before and having financed such retaliations in the past, Jackson's new colleagues repaid Tennessee handsomely—$20,000 for defense, not one cent for razed fruit trees.

Congressional service confirmed Jackson's belief that personal loyalty was the essence of politics. He had risen to political prominence by faithfully serving William Blount—fighting his legal battles, representing him in the militia, defending his filibustering schemes, agreeing to serve out his senatorial term. The national party structure offered Jackson no such rewards. He entered Congress at a time when parties were still in a formative stage, when they took shape from legislative maneuvering, not from movements within the states. Jackson lacked the personality and temperament to prosper in such a system. He could not inspire men with his oratory. Never skilled in public speaking, Jackson was awkward, his gestures graceless, his voice high-pitched. Anger was his most effective weapon for it bore the imprint of conviction; but when angry, he had to guard against the excesses of temper—the blurted statements, the breakdown of civility, the rash remarks. Surrounded in the Senate by men who had mastered the art of polemical persuasion, Jackson felt insecure. If demagoguery was to be the essential ingredient for partisan success, Jackson wanted no part of party. Nor did he have the patience for the subtle diplomacy, the parliamentary protocol so necessary for legislative alliances. The unhappy senator resigned his post in 1798, convinced, as were many of his contemporaries, that national parties were run by unscrupulous, unprincipled men solely for the sake of aggrandizement and intrigue.

Resignation in no way injured Jackson's political standing in Tennessee. Thankful for the opportunity to appoint yet another of its members to the U.S. Senate, the Blount regime granted Jackson his cherished judgeship at $600 per year. The ex-senator enthusiastically accepted the state post and the sub-stantial income. For the next six years he remained on the bench, rendering a crude but fair brand of justice.

Jackson was a popular judge; a number of prominent citi-zens petitioned him to reconsider his decision to resign in 1804. He kept the dockets clean, insisted on respect for the law, and was not intimidated by frontier violence. Jackson earned a measure of respect from his judicial colleagues as well. He looked every bit a judge—tall, lean, haughty. A good many defendants, already terrified by the courtroom, no doubt found him frightening and wavered under his intense gaze, all to the delight of the lawyers who accompanied him on the circuit, for they knew the judge had other manners. In the excitement of the cockpits and the conviviality of the tavern, they saw a different Andrew Jackson, more relaxed, more out-going, more friendly. If Jackson wearied of the circuit, he never complained. In his travels he made new friends and kept himself in public view. Such visibility was vitally important in an age when communications were so primitive that an itiner-ant judge could become as popular as a sedentary governor. Popularity had its price: the extended absences troubled Ra-chel, who pleaded with her husband not to tarry so long. Although he retired from the bench in 1804, Jackson contin-ued to trade on his judicial reputation for years to come.

Fame, Jackson discovered, did not automatically lead to for-tune. For nearly a decade he had been involved in an uphill battle for economic survival. As a judge, he earned a salary second only to that of the governor, but frontier fortunes did not spring from steady income. Land brought the highest re-wards and Jackson, along with other members of the Tennes-see elite, speculated heavily. Such speculation followed a definite pattern. After buying land in Tennessee, an entre-preneur would travel east to Philadelphia, sell the land in return for plantation supplies, bear the cost of transporting these back to the Cumberland, and then hope to sell them at a reasonable profit. At the same time another trade cycle operated. Tennessee planters needed a market for their crops. Since there was no adequate way to transport them to the east, they would consign them to a Nashville agent, who would ship them to New Orleans and recover profits from the sale. Simple in theory, the two operations contained numerous pitfalls. Payments often came in farm produce; some never came at all. There was also a delicate timing in all of this. The unwary creditor without sufficient financial resources might ride the crest of prosperity one year, only to crash into debt the next. These harsh realities Jackson learned as a young man.

After establishing a law practice and concluding an advantageous marriage, Jackson set out in pursuit of fortune. Together with his good friend John Overton, he accumulated nearly 50,000 acres of land. Overton knew title law and was a shrewd manipulator, yet in 1795 he let Jackson make the trip to Philadelphia to sell the property. The inexperienced young speculator spent over three weeks trying to find a buyer. Overwhelmed with details, Jackson found himself in the "dam'st situation ever man was placed in." In desperation he concluded a bargain with a former Tennessee entrepreneur, David Allison, whose notes he took to two Philadelphia merchants and there purchased supplies for a new store in Nashville. The complexities seemed endless. The freight bill alone came to $644.86 and included payments to three cargo carriers, purchase of a flatboat, hire of a crew, and fees to three intermediary agents. Exhausted, Jackson returned home to set up his store, only to learn that Allison had defaulted on the notes. "We shall have to get the money from you," read the ominous letter from the Philadelphia mercantile firm of Meeker and Cochran. For the next ten years Jackson struggled to meet demands such as these. As he did, the excitement, the eagerness of ambition gave way to the gnawing fear of debt.

The Allison affair had a profound impact on Jackson's financial outlook, but it did not make him an implacable foe of paper money and banks. As a planter and erstwhile merchant, he continued to rely on credit; the structure of the western economy gave him no choice. Nor did he abandon financial intrigue or shun the company of speculators. While still extricating himself from the Allison debts, Jackson thought of raising $40,000 for the purchase of a salt deposit on the Illinois River. His agent in this venture was John Coffee, a large handsome Virginian who later married Rachel's niece. The saline empire never materialized, but Jackson and Coffee became business partners, fast friends, and eventually comrades in arms.

Jackson abhorred debt and fought to avoid being victimized by forces beyond his control. But some inner compulsion drove him to make further investment. Retrenchment and frugality were garments he wore later in life, and then more for public display than private comfort. Though he might preach economic repentance, Jackson was always something of a gambler at heart. This trait was most evident in his passion for horse racing.

Although early nineteenth-century Americans needed horses for domestic purposes, few raised them for the track. Many of Jackson's contemporaries shared his enthusiasm for proper horse breeding but were convinced that racing destroyed an animal's endurance. Of those who did breed racers, few trained them as hard or demanded as much as Andrew Jackson. Neither financial misfortune, the horrors of war, nor the pressures of the presidency made him forget racing. This obsession affords another glimpse of Jackson's personality. As a prudent man, he left little to chance, purchasing the best horses he could afford, following a strict training regimen, and employing experienced jockeys. Dedication, hard work, and discipline was the formula for victory, if not in economic affairs, then certainly in racing. Although such prudence reduced the odds, it could not eliminate all risks. In risks lay all the rewards. The prospect of instant personal triumph of a sort rarely possible in social affairs—there was the allure. The race was immediate; in that short circle of time a man could prove himself anew.

Jackson invested heavily at the track—of himself and of his resources. As a young man in Charleston he had casually thrown the dice to escape a landlord's wrath; now, with prosperity and status at stake, he gambled in earnest. In 1805, mired in debt, his mercantile operations floundering despite John Coffee's devoted assistance, Jackson somehow raised enough money to purchase a prize stallion named Truxton. After intensive, grueling training, Jackson entered his new horse in a race against the season's reigning champion, Greyhound. The meeting attracted widespread attention and enormous wagers. Entire sections of land, dozens of horses, whole wardrobes of clothes rode on the outcome. Jackson himself gambled $5,000. His dedication and horse sense prevailed— going away. Jackson accepted the victory calmly and immediately entered Truxton in the fall races; his stallion compiled an outstanding record. Enriched by fat purses, public acclaim, and substantial stud fees, Jackson looked forward to a more peaceful and secure future.

Still the challenges would not cease and Andrew Jackson was not a man to accept challenge calmly. In the spring of 1806, the scene shifted from the race course to the dueling ground. His opponent was Charles Dickinson, a twenty-seven-year-old gentleman reputed to have been the best shot in Tennessee. The issues now seem petty, especially as printed on the yellowing pages of the *Impartial Review and Cumberland Repository.* Jackson had niggled about the details of a race forfeiture; Dickinson, while intoxicated, made irreverent remarks about Rachel, for which he later apologized. Reasonable men might have compromised. Yet the atmosphere was too charged, the interests too great, and the principals too headstrong for impartial review. Disappointed at the track, Dickinson hoped to gain recognition by the duel; marksmanship alone put the odds in his favor. Jackson might have dissuaded his young opponent by private diplomacy; yet he rose to the challenge, rushing into print to defend himself. For in assailing Jackson's honor, in raising the issue of feminine virtue, Dickinson had trod on sacred ground. The unseemly exchange dragged on for months and soon encompassed Jackson's political reputation and standing in the community. One taunting correspondent called Jackson a coward, more willing to shed "*bushels of ink* than one ounce of blood." No legal mechanism could resolve this conflict, not when it involved overweening ambition and such a deep sense of injured pride. The time had come for the two gentlemen to give each other satisfaction.

They chose a site north of Nashville, just across the Kentucky border. Enroute to the dueling ground, Jackson's friends discussed possible strategies. John Overton apparently convinced his friend to wear a loose-fitting coat; with the duelists standing sideways, the garment might disguise Jackson's slender frame, thus spoiling Dickinson's aim. Jackson listened to this advice but little else. He had already decided to let his opponent have the first shot, knowing full well that Dickinson could scarcely miss at the murderous distance of twenty-four feet. Then, even though hit, Jackson believed he could take deliberate aim and return the fire. Considering Dickinson's reputation, such a strategy was incredibly heroic and foolhardy. But Jackson's manner was not that of a hero or a fool; he was strangely silent, perhaps listening to other voices, other advice. "If ever you have to vindicate your feelings or your honor, do it calmly," his mother had said. "Avoid quarrels as long as you can, but sustain your manhood always." Jackson was about to tempt death again, but this time he was prepared. Dickinson's bullet might snuff out his life, but it would make his reputation immortal.

Shortly after sunrise on the morning of May 30, 1806, the duelists took their appointed positions. No sooner had Overton yelled "fire" than Dickinson snapped off a shot, raising a puff of dust from Jackson's billowing coat. The tall, slender figure clutched his chest, but remained standing. "Great God have I missed him?" Dickinson screamed, recoiling in shock. Ordered back to the mark, he trembled as Jackson raised to fire. The pistol stopped at half cock—a miraculous reprieve. In some dueling circles this amounted to a shot, but not this day, not while Jackson was silently spilling blood, fearful that his life might be slipping away. Overton ordered Dickinson to stand again, and this time Jackson's pistol did not fail him. The bullet tore into Dickinson's abdomen and he fell to the ground. Within twelve hours he would bleed to death. Jackson retired, carefully concealing his own wound from Dickinson's retainers. Triumphant, maddened with pain, he would give no further satisfaction; he had already given quite enough.

Nashville neither honored Jackson's courage nor celebrated his return. The *Impartial Review* "went into mourning," its black-bordered columns reprinting angry letters denouncing Dickinson's "murder." As he slowly recovered from his narrow brush with death, Jackson reacted bitterly to the charges. His quarrel with Dickinson had been a private matter; the public had no business judging a gentleman's affairs. Jackson's outrage concealed much deeper insecurity and confusion. He could not understand the public response, not when he had gone to such lengths to seek vindication. The protests in the paper concerned the details of the duel and gave no assessment of Dickinson's character. In Jackson's opinion, Dickinson was a social upstart who showed no respect for his elders, little concern for propriety, and no appreciation for social stability. Jackson believed that the duel was socially justified as a mechanism for restoring order.

By the time Jackson left the dueling ground he had come to hate Charles Dickinson. "I should have hit him," Jackson boasted, "if he had shot me through the brain." Jackson even went to the extreme of charging the dead man with slave trading, a morally offensive traffic to slave owners with ambivalent attitudes toward the peculiar institution. Why Jackson felt so strongly remains a mystery. Certainly he was capable of hatred; his feeling always ran to such extremes. But why Charles Dickinson? No stranger to swaggering, dueling, or slave trading, Jackson probably saw something of himself in his young opponent—some unpleasant reminder of the inse-

cure past. Jackson felt no guilt in punishing Dickinson's inso-
lence, not when it stemmed from the very defects of character
that Jackson had vowed to uproot. The public could not appreciate these private feelings. They did not attend the duel, did
not see the hatred, did not understand the source of Jackson's
anxieties. They saw only the results: a young man killed in the
prime of his life by one who epitomized the law in a society
plagued by lawlessness. They buried Charles Dickinson and
with him a large measure of Jackson's social standing.

III

Martial Fame

THE REPUTATION THAT JACKSON lost on the field of honor he regained on the field of battle. He had practically no military experience, but then he had grown up in a society that abhorred standing armies and expected little training of military leaders. Citizen soldiers, like the minutemen of old, were equal to any challenge; generals, like Cincinnatus, could put down the plow and take up the sword. Throughout his military career, Jackson paid lip service to these cherished republican ideals. Privately, he identified more with conquering generals than citizen soldiers. In 1798, he secretly hoped that Napoleon would invade England, for then "Tyranny will be humbled, a throne crushed and a republic will spring from the wreck, and millions of distressed people restored to the rights of man by the conquering army of Bonaparte."

Jackson entered politics to become a judge; he played politics to become a general. Through the influence of the Blount faction, Jackson had won appointment as judge advocate of the militia; in 1796, he set his sights on the post of major general, the highest military office in Tennessee. Immediately he ran into opposition from the incumbent, John Sevier, who was being forced by the new state constitution to relinquish the position before assuming duties as governor. The crusty old revolutionary veteran found divestiture difficult, especially when his potential successor was Blount's protégé and but a "poor pitiful petty fogging lawyer." Sevier resented men like

Jackson and was impolitic enough to say so, even to the extent of interfering in the election. Jackson lost the election and blaming Sevier, embarked on a personal campaign of revenge. Over the next four years, he collected evidence of Sevier's role in a vast scandal that involved forging military land warrants.

In 1801, Jackson saw his chance. His friend Archibald Roane was elected governor, and Jackson again became a candidate for major general. This time John Sevier opposed him personally. The young judge and the old verteran ran a dead heat; Roane broke the tie by selecting Jackson. Loyalty to the Blount faction no doubt dictated Roane's decision, but he also had reason to be grateful to Jackson: on the very day of the militia election, Jackson had delivered documents detailing Sevier's misconduct. He was even willing to jeopardize the Donelson name, for his evidence proved that Rachel's brother Stockley was deeply involved in the scandal.

Sevier retaliated, but not as Jackson anticipated. The ex-governor's adherents persuaded the legislature to cut the military district in two, thus drastically reducing Jackson's power. To add insult to injury, Sevier won the gubernatorial race in 1803, despite the publication of Jackson's charges. During the campaign the two men came to blows, of sorts, occasioned by Sevier's public charge that Jackson "had run off with another man's wife." Some insults the new major general could not bear. Frantically, Jackson appealed to the code of honor. Hastily, Sevier declined, claiming that his courage was beyond suspicion. Jackson then proclaimed Sevier a "base coward and poltroon," rode into Indian country, and waited for his opponent to come and give him satisfaction. Sevier finally rose to the challenge, but the confrontation proved more dodge than duel. Both men drew pistols, then put them away; Jackson brandished a sword; Sevier hid behind a tree. Their seconds nearly came to blows before the farce finally ended with no shots exchanged, nor much satisfaction either.

There was meaning behind this madness. The clash of personalities obscured a much more significant confrontation over the nature and purpose of the militia. To Sevier, the militia was a deterrent to future Indian attacks as well as an adjunct to diplomacy. A veteran of more than a score of battles, he resented turning over control to officers with no combat experience. Jackson, too, appreciated the need for vigilance, but he belonged to a generation that had come to power in more peaceful times. He saw great political potential in the ranks of the citizen soldiery. In each county, the wealthiest planters served as colonels in addition to holding the prominent offices of local government. Command of the Tennessee militia thus allied Jackson with the most powerful and prominent men in the state. Jackson marshaled this political strength effectively, retaining his appointment despite public disapproval of his attacks on Sevier. By contrast, Sevier could always rely on enormous popular support to win election as governor, no matter how inept his politics.

Jackson risked his newly acquired commission by plunging into an even more Byzantine embroglio—the Burr conspiracy. Few episodes in American history are so famous, so confusing, so bizarre. In bare outline, the plot looks simple. Disgruntled, former vice-president Aaron Burr visited Tennessee in 1805 to recruit support for an unspecified military campaign against the Spanish. His agent and host in Nashville, Andrew Jackson, agreed to provide troops and supplies in the event of war. Unfortunately, Burr's other military ally, James Wilkinson, turned traitor and wrote the president that Burr's true intent was to divide the Union and establish a personal empire. Understandably agitated, Thomas Jefferson issued instructions for Burr's arrest. At the subsequent trial, Burr was acquitted and the nature of his alleged treason left to the mercy of historical speculation.

Most of Jackson's biographers have acquitted the major general as well. They admit that he contracted to build Burr's boats and to supply him in the event of war, but they insist this agreement reflected Jackson's nationalistic hatred of the Spanish, not his own personal ambition. According to these accounts, Burr, the wily deceiver, lulled Jackson with assurances of federal sponsorship. Taken in for a time, Jackson finally awoke in the fall of 1806 and rushed to the defense of the Union. "The possibility of treason by Andrew Jackson is utterly impossible," says his most recent biographer. The nineteenth-century frontiersman, however, was not so quick to define filibustering or private diplomacy with a foreign power as treasonous. Jackson certainly was no stranger to such intrigue, having eagerly participated in the Spanish conspiracy in 1789 and having loyally served his patron William Blount, whose conniving brought expulsion from the Senate. Nor is it likely that Jackson fell prey to Burr's charms; as a young congressman he never stood in awe of the nation's first president, why should he be duped by its third vice-president?

More likely, Jackson supported Burr's schemes, vague and ill-defined as they were. The idea of a field command must have appealed to a man whose military credentials had so recently come under attack. Jackson made a strategic retreat in the fall of 1806, yet surely not because he had suddenly learned of Burr's dalliance with disunion; the former vice-president's motives had been rumored for some time. What startled Jackson was the report that he was not to be Burr's main military ally; that dubious honor was to go to James Wilkinson, a schemer of great guile. This came as a severe blow to Jackson's martial pretensions. Still, despite proof that Burr was up to no good, Jackson delivered the boats as promised and even allowed Rachel's nephew to join the entourage. Only a federal warrant for Burr's arrest dissuaded Jackson from further involvement.

Abruptly, the spurned suitor became the outspoken patriot. Jackson dashed off letters to Washington, assuring Secretary of War Henry Dearborn that he stood ready to "quell the conspiracy, resting confident that the government will sanction my conduct." Dearborn had not the slightest intention of sanctioning the hot-headed militia commander or of enlisting his services. Jackson resented the snub. "The Secretary of War is not fit for a granny," he wrote angrily. He desperately wanted to be on the march—against Spain, against Burr, against someone. The longer he remained inactive, the more vulnerable he felt. Action would purge the public mind and remove all doubts of his loyalty. The orders never came and, by the time of Burr's trial in the spring of 1807, Jackson imagined a vast plot involving Wilkinson, Dearborn, and even the president, all bent on ruining his reputation.

Jackson never turned on the man most responsible for his predicament. He continued to protest Burr's innocence, thereby asserting his own as well. Such posturing was not sheer hypocrisy, for Jackson's emotions ran deep and to extremes. "I am more convinced than ever that Treason never was intended by Burr," Jackson said at the time of the trial, "but if ever it was, you know my wishes that he may be hung."

Already suspected of having private military ambitions, Jackson only increased official distrust by his constant pleas for preparedness and his criticisms of the militia system. He drafted proposals for a federal training program, urged an end to the election of officers, and claimed that with proper organization and support, Tennessee could develop an army that would be able "to oppose with success Bonaparte's legions." Jackson relished war with England, as it would end the "scenes of corruption" in the regular army command and eliminate the "temporizing spirit that appears to pervade Congress." It would, moreover, avenge "the many degredations and insults our country has rec'd." He firmly believed that war would rescue the nation's honor, not to mention his own faltering reputation.

In the spring of 1812, all signs indicated that Andrew Jackson and other "War Hawks" would have their wish. Not that the nation had been suddenly persuaded by Western propaganda; the country was far too fragmented for any single group or section to exercise such influence. The United States went to war in 1812 because it was too proud to admit that it was a weak maritime nation, lacking the naval forces to defend its neutral rights. Ever since the waning years of Jefferson's second term, the Republican leadership had tried to avenge a series of diplomatic disasters, ranging from Britain's economic strangulation to the impressment of American seamen. In the late spring of 1812, the Madison administration yielded to the strident appeals to national conscience and embarked on "the Second and last struggle for national freedom." The country had its rhetoric ready but little else.

Jackson was prepared even though the nation was not. In anticipation of the declaration of war, he issued a grandiose proclamation exhorting "volunteers to arms." The call combined an appeal to national honor with oblique reminders that even the institution of slavery might come under attack. He also held out to the potential recruits the possibility of "a military promenade into some distant country"—say Canada —where they could "tread the consecrated spot on which Wolf and Montgomery fell."

Having issued his appeal, he waited impatiently for orders. In early June 1812, a week before the official declaration of war, he tried to persuade the governor to authorize a punitive expedition against the Creek Indians. "When we figure to ourselves our beloved wives and little prattling infants, butchered, mangled, murdered, and torn to pieces by savage bloodhounds, and wallowing in their gore, you can judge of our feelings." The governor knew Jackson's feelings quite well and issued no authorization. Prevented from punishing the Creeks, Jackson turned his wrath in another direction.

His target was Silas Dinsmore, an agent to the Choctaw Indians in the Mississippi territory. Jackson distrusted men like Dinsmore who represented a peaceful approach to red–white relations. "Fear is better than love with an Indian," Jackson observed on more than one occasion. Yet it was not Dinsmore's ministrations to the Choctaws that angered Jackson. In 1811, in response to the demands of several planters, Dinsmore took steps to prevent runaway slaves from using the

Choctaw settlement as a refuge. He began to enforce a congressional act requiring all who passed through Indian territory to show passports. In addition, white travelers had to present papers proving that the blacks in their company were not runaways. This practice angered transient planters accustomed to having their mastery taken for granted.

Soon Jackson stumbled into the controversy. Rumors reached Nashville that one of Rachel's young cousins, sent to New Orleans to sell slaves, was mismanaging the sales and squandering the proceeds. Jackson rushed south, rounded up the remaining slaves, and headed home. By the time he reached Dinsmore's checkpoint he was in no mood for a challenge. Brandishing a rifle, he marched into the agency, only to find Dinsmore away. Upon his return to Nashville, Jackson bragged that he had successfully defied the Choctaw agent, thereby crippling the abhorrent search procedure and reestablishing the rights of slave owners to uninterrupted travel.

In September 1812, Jackson discovered that Dinsmore had no intention of backing down and had gone so far as to detain a woman traveling with her ten Negroes. Jackson immediately demanded Dinsmore's removal; in the process the irate general revealed the depths and complexity of his desire to wage war. In a rambling, unrestrained, and almost incoherent letter to his congressman, Jackson poured out his frustrations. Before Congress had even declared war, Jackson had rushed to defend "those independent rights secured to us by the bravery and blood of our forefathers." Among those rights, that of owning slaves was of paramount importance. British aggression threatened that right and all other rights of property. Jackson took this threat quite personally; once before, in 1781, the British had invaded his world, leaving him an orphan. Thwarted in his attempt to revenge that invasion, Jackson struck out blindly at Dinsmore, who, like the British, seemed bent on "lawless tyranny." "My God; is it come to this," Jackson asked in disbelief, "are we *free men or are we slaves . . . is this real or is it a dream*—for what are we involved in a War with great Britain if it is not for the support of our rights as an independent people. . . ."

To further aggravate matters, Dinsmore had practiced his "lawless tyranny" "over a helpless and unprotected female." The insult challenged Jackson's sense of "Patriotism and gallantry." He would never forget that the last war had taken another "helpless and unprotected female" and left him an orphan, tormented by ambivalent feelings about his own mortality. Since then, he had struggled to give meaning to that sacrifice, to conquer his secret fears. Now with the enemy once more at the gates, the awful ambivalence returned: "Are we *free men or are we slaves. . . . is this real or is it a dream. . . .*" Jackson desperately wanted reassurance, for these questions were as fundamental as life and death. If he could not attack the British or assault the Creeks, at least he could silence one "source of evil." "We love order," he pledged, but if the government did not rouse itself from its slumber, "the agent, and his houses will be demolished." Fortunately for Silas Dinsmore, Jackson soon received marching orders.

Even in the call to arms, Jackson saw his enemies at work. In November 1812, he was ordered to march his troops to New Orleans. He fully appreciated the wisdom of the move but found the necessity of reporting to his nemesis General James Wilkinson "a bitter pill . . . but for my country's good I will swallow." Jackson's apprehension may help explain the inherent contradictions in his final messages to his soldiers, contradictions that did not augur well for future order and discipline. The new major general spoke of winning great glory but hoped his "brave volunteers" would not "prove themselves a degenerate race." While admiring their "honorable zeal," he warned that any who strayed would be subject to the "severest penalties which the laws will inflict upon him." As for his own responsibilities, Jackson promised to act like "a father to his family. Your *moral duty* as soldiers," he told the troops, "is subordination." Having defined his patriarchal authority, Jackson concluded by exulting, "United as a band of brothers we will overcome all opposition." Sons, brothers, he had neither. In his farewell letters Jackson had this emptiness very much in mind as he recalled another war against the "tyranny of Britain" that had cost him "everything that was dear to me, my *brothers and my fortune.*"

The journey that began with great expectations ended in utter despair. Jackson reached Natchez in mid-February 1813 and spent the next month waiting for official clarification of the relationship between his command and Wilkinson's. Then came an incredible letter from John Armstrong, the new secretary of war, dismissing Jackson's troops and ordering him to turn over "to Major General Wilkinson all articles of public property. . . . You will accept for yourself and the corps the thanks of the president of the United States." Thanks indeed! Even the timing conspired to insult; dispatched early in February, the order arrived on Jackson's forty-sixth birthday.

Jackson promptly protested. Although he agreed to give up some government property, he refused to dismiss his troops, fearing that they would fall prey to "petty recruiting officers." No, he would march them back to Nashville, through eight hundred miles of "savage land"; there and there only would he relinquish command. Having told the secretary of war what he thought of the order, Jackson wrote directly to the president: "I cannot believe [the] thing was ever written by your direction or knowledge." While he marched back to Nashville, Jackson's disbelief turned to brooding suspicion as he envisioned a vast conspiracy to undermine his military reputation.

Jackson's disgust overcame his better judgment. Shortly after reaching Nashville, he meddled in a private quarrel involving members of his staff. Brigade Inspector William Carroll, one of Jackson's favorite staff members and hence the envy of disappointed spoils seekers, refused a call for a duel on grounds that his challenger was not a gentleman. Whereupon Jesse Benton, whose brother Thomas Hart Benton was also a Jackson aide, renewed the challenge. Carroll then asked Jackson to be his second. The general demurred, claiming that he was too old for such affairs, but Jesse Benton's taunts soon drove him to distraction and he relented. The duel was even more farcical than Jackson's encounter with Sevier. The opponents lined up ten feet apart but stood back to back instead of facing each other. On signal they wheeled to fire. Benton snapped off a shot and then, in a moment of panic, crouched to avoid being hit. Carroll returned the fire and struck Benton squarely in the rump.

Both Benton and Jackson had been caught in embarrassing positions. The code of honor never entitled a gentleman to crouch, nor did the military code encourage a general to stoop so low as to interfere in the personal affairs of his staff. To confuse matters, Jesse's brother Thomas was running a military errand for Jackson and was in Washington at the time of the fracas. When he returned, Benton openly criticized Jackson's part in the affair. Jackson in turn defended the duel but warned Benton not to pursue matters further. "It is the character of a man of honor not to quarrel and brawl like a fish woman," Jackson instructed his young critic. But brawl they did as Jackson attacked Benton in a Nashville hotel, screaming, "Now you damned rascal, I'm going to punish you! Defend yourself!" Benton stumbled down a hallway with Jackson in hot pursuit, when suddenly brother Jesse leaped out of a doorway (where he had been crouching?) and discharged his pistol directly into Jackson's shoulder. Onlookers ended the melee. The brothers escaped and public indignation forced them to leave town, costing Thomas Hart Benton a promising military career.

By precipitating this fight, Jackson risked his life at the very moment that war threatened to break out in earnest. Three weeks before he sallied into the Nashville hotel, Jackson had been warned of a massive Indian uprising and ordered to place the militia on alert. No doubt he considered the attack on Benton as a kind of preparation—a settlement of accounts, a proof of courage. He had barely begun to recuperate when word reached Nashville that the Creek Indians were on the warpath.

South of Tennessee, the thriving Creek confederation controlled three hundred square miles of the most fertile land in the deep South. White settlers had long coveted this region. Through it ran the Coosa and Tallapoosa Rivers, which united to form the Alabama, the main artery to Mobile and the Gulf Coast. In the eighteenth century the Creeks discovered that their only hope for survival lay in alliances with America's enemies, first Spain, then England. Despite this assistance, the Creeks were not well armed. No more than a quarter of the four thousand warriors had guns and ammunition, yet they determined to take advantage of America's military preoccupations. Early in 1813, Creek warriors joined British soldiers in a successful northern campaign. Emboldened by this victory, the upper portion of the Creek confederation decided on war. On August 30, 1813, they attacked Fort Mims, a white outpost forty-five miles north of Mobile.

Weakened by considerable loss of blood and maddened by a painful fracture that nearly cost him his left arm, Jackson learned of the Fort Mims "massacre" in mid-September. A more prudent, less determined man might have relinquished command, but Jackson told anxious bedside visitors that he would return to the field as soon as possible. He promptly issued orders calling for "retaliatory vengeance" against "those inhuman bloodthirsty barbarians."

His soldiers needed a definition of their enlistment contracts more than impassioned appeals. A majority of the volunteers had originally enlisted on December 10, 1812, under a congressional act setting the maximum term of service at one year, unless discharged sooner. Jackson had actually issued such a discharge after the retreat from Natchez in the spring of 1813, but only to allow his men to retain the arms they had been issued. In return, they agreed informally to remain on call until the expiration of their enlistments in December 1813. Almost to a man, the volunteers honored their promises when the Creek war erupted; almost to a man they expected to return home on the anniversary of their original muster. Jackson had other ideas. He believed that the volunteers should serve an additional six months to compensate for their summer idleness. As a former judge, he certainly knew that the volunteers had the law on their side; as a general, he hoped that early December would find his army victorious or so deep in Indian country as to discourage releases. Jackson should have resolved this conflict before heading South, for it would eventually cause him more pain than Jesse Benton's bullet.

Having long anticipated the Creek uprising, the federal government had formulated an elaborate strategy. Jackson was to lead his 2,500 troops into the heart of the Creek nation and there join forces from East Tennessee and Georgia. The three-pronged attack envisioned far more coordination than the primitive transportation system could bear, which was to Jackson's advantage. Let others "await the slow and tardy orders of the general govt"; he intended to seek out and destroy the enemy as soon as possible, with or without additional support. After cutting a military road from the Tennessee River across the Lookout Mountains to the banks of the Coosa, Jackson built his base camp, Fort Strother, and immediately went on the offensive. On November 2, 1813, he ordered his cavalry commander, John Coffee, to take one thousand men and attack Tallushatchee, a Creek town thirteen miles to the east. Early the next morning, Coffee's men invaded the village. "The General executed this order in stile," Jackson proudly reported. "A hundred and eighty six of the enemy were found dead on the field and eighty taken prisoner." Jackson was far too excited to notice the women and children who died in the attack. "We have retaliated for the destruction at Fort Mims," he exclaimed. But not completely. Not yet.

As soon as Coffee returned to camp, Jackson set out to strike another Indian force, thirty miles to the south. His spies claimed that over a thousand Creeks were massed around the friendly village of Talledega. By the evening of November 8, Jackson had approached to within six miles of the enemy and in hurried conferences with his staff decided to lure the Indians into a trap. He would deploy his infantry in the center of a crescent-shaped line of battle, his cavalry on the wings. A small militia force would advance and draw the Indians into an attack on the center of the line. The cavalry would thus be free to encircle the exposed Creek assault. Shortly after sunrise the following morning, Jackson had his troops in position. The Creeks responded to the first militia charge as Jackson predicted; soon the Indians headed directly toward the concealed main force. The cavalry closed in. For a time it appeared that all the warriors would perish, when suddenly they discovered a gap in the line and nearly two-thirds of them escaped. Although angry about this breach, Jackson took satisfaction in counting nearly three hundred Indian dead. He reported his own losses as fifteen killed and eighty-five wounded, and he claimed that "no impartial man can say that a more splendid result has in any instance attended our arms, *on land,* since the commencement of the war."

Jackson had good reason to boast, for in two successive engagements he had demonstrated considerable tactical skill. For a general with no previous combat experience, this was quite remarkable. Jackson's instincts and temperament were exceptionally well suited to aggressive, frontier war-making. If he had a flaw as a tactician, it was excessive boldness, not unlike his spirited gambling at the race track. In marching to Talledega, for instance, Jackson left Fort Strother almost totally defenseless in anticipation of the arrival of reinforcements from East Tennessee. Even when he learned they would not arrive and that his wounded men and supplies were in jeopardy, Jackson went ahead with his attack. Under pressure, he had the ability to make up his mind quickly. When in complete command of a battlefield situation, Jackson was extremely adept at directing troop placements, anticipating the enemy's movements, and modifying his plan of attack. What bothered him as a general had bothered him since adolescence: the forces beyond his control.

Though successful in battle, Jackson never devised a strategy to solve the numerous logistical problems that plagued his army after it left Tennessee. He had outstripped his supplies. The army relied upon inefficient civilian contractors, many of whom valued self-preservation above profit. Jackson, who had vowed to march south even if he had to "live upon acorns," changed contractors several times, burned down Indian villages in search of rations, and still could not provision his base camp. The critical shortages soon produced widespread discontent among the troops, who warned of "a forcible and tumultuous desertion of the camp."

The discipline mustered at Talledega broke down entirely in the face of starvation. Jackson suddenly seemed powerless. At first he received petitions with utter contempt. If he could live on acorns, why couldn't his men? Twice his soldiers began to leave the fort; twice he forced them back. Then the embittered general vacillated. Hearing that supplies were finally on the way, he made a symbolic concession: if two days passed without provisions, he vowed to sound the retreat. His gamble failed; the supplies did not arrive. Reluctantly, Jackson headed home. Twelve miles north of Fort Strother, his column met the contractors with a herd of cattle. Jackson allowed his soldiers to slaughter some of the animals and have their fill, then he promptly ordered a return to the fort. When one company refused, Jackson personally grabbed a musket and threatened to shoot any man who made a move toward Tennessee. No one volunteered. Boldness ended the mutiny but not the discontent.

As soon as the disgruntled troops returned to Fort Strother, the volunteers gave notice that they expected to be discharged on December 10, the anniversary of their original enlistments. The general who once defied the federal government to keep his soldiers in service now claimed he had no authority to let them go and promised to refer the matter to Washington. Clearly Jackson was gambling for time to avoid losing over half his army. The volunteers reminded him that they had only returned to the field because they expected release on December 10, that they had left home hurriedly without proper clothing, and that they had the law on their side. Determined to go, they wanted "to part with their general with that cordiality, with which they had served. together."

Their general was hardly cordial on the eve of December 10, the night the brigade intended to leave camp. Having tried every subterfuge and legal stratagem he knew, having appealed to patriotism and honor, having threatened them with disgrace, Jackson was exhausted and in an ugly mood. He arrayed loyal militia units on one side of the fort, wheeled two cannons into line, and then ordered the dissident brigade to parade in front of the guns. He harangued them, challenging them to desert or give up their rebellion. When they remained silent, he brought the cannons to bear; the gunners lighted their matches. Finally the volunteers backed down and agreed to remain in camp. After winning this dramatic war of nerves, Jackson seemed to give up. On December 14, 1813, he allowed the volunteers to return to Nashville.

By the end of the month, Jackson was desperate and on the verge of losing his entire command. One unit after another demanded discharge. Even the soldiers recruited in October brandished guarantees that promised release within three months. Grudgingly, Jackson signed the orders, rationalizing that sedition had so lowered morale that the defectors would be useless in the field. Still, he steadfastly ignored suggestions that he turn back to the Tennessee River to await reinforcements.

The obstinacy concealed despair unlike any he had known for more than thirty years. In 1814 Andrew Jackson was a sick man. His wound was healing slowly; he contracted dysentery and was often so wracked by convulsions that he doubled over a sapling to ease the pain. Physical agony increased both his determination and his despondency. To Jackson the war was not a matter of contracts, terms of service, or dates of discharge, but a campaign to vindicate national honor and to prove his personal worth by triumphing over the enemy's wickedness. With victory almost assured, "mutiny and sedition stalked in my army." "My army": there was the key. Unable to understand why "his children" had disobeyed authority, Jackson cast about for scapegoats. He found several: the contractors, the governor, the volunteer officers—especially the officers "who wish to raise their popularity by my downfall."

By the beginning of the new year, with Fort Strother all but abandoned, Jackson felt desolated. It was in this mood that he wrote to Rachel inquiring about Lincoya, a three-year-old Creek Indian boy he had found on a deserted battlefield in November and sent to Nashville. Jackson intended Lincoya as a playmate for his other adopted son. "Keep Lincoya in the house—he is savage," Jackson told Rachel. Then, softening a bit, he wondered whether the child had "been given to me for some valuable purpose—in fact when I reflect that he as to his relations is so much like myself I feel an unusual bond of sympathy for him." Not so unusual perhaps, not to a man who desperately needed proof that he too had been saved for "some valuable purpose."

The private anger and suspicion ran so deep that they eventually colored official correspondence. In a letter to the governor of Tennessee, Jackson exploded: "Arouse from yr. lethargy . . . with energy exercise yr. functions—the campaign must rapidly progress, or you are forever damned, and yr. country ruined." The governor wisely overlooked the intemperate remarks; he could not afford the political consequences of removing a general who had vowed to "carry the *campaign into* the heart of the *Creek nation* and *exterminate them*" and who in two successive engagements had proven himself equal to that task. Instead of taking offense the governor and some of the discharged officers, who had also been the targets of Jackson's rage, helped enlist new recruits. By Jackson's forty-seventh birthday, Fort Strother contained a full complement of 5,000 men. The joy of seeing reinforcements was sweetened by letters from Rachel, one of which enclosed some verse:

Ha: methinks thy glances reading,
From thine eyes my fate I know.
Duty still love's claim impeding
Thou again must seek the foe.

Jackson had no difficulty finding his foe in the spring of 1814. Having suffered severe casualties in two running battles in the fall, the Creeks decided to barricade themselves on the Tallapoosa River in an area called Horse Shoe Bend. The name was appropriate. The Creeks occupied a peninsula formed by a large loop in the river. Breastworks across the neck of the peninsula provided excellent cover for their riflemen. At the far end of the encampment, on the banks of the river, they built their village, drawing their canoes up on the shore for emergency evacuation. The entire complex covered nearly a hundred acres. Over a thousand warriors crowded inside along with three hundred women and children.

Jackson approached Horse Shoe Bend on the morning of March 27 with nearly three thousand men, including friendly Creeks and Cherokees. Jackson stationed Coffee on the opposite bank of the river to cut off any avenue of escape. From this position the friendly Indians swam across, entered the village, destroyed canoes, and burned the huts. At the same time Jackson's infantry began its assault on the breastworks. The battle raged for nearly five hours; the militia successfully stormed the log fortress and pushed the Creeks back up the peninsula. "The *carnage* was *dreadful,*" Jackson later admitted. "Five hundred and fifty-seven were found by officers of great respectability whom I ordered to count them." Jackson also reported that nearly three hundred Creeks had drowned or been shot trying to escape. His own losses amounted to 59 killed and 150 wounded.

Having given no quarter in battle, Jackson gave none in peace. He did not seem unduly troubled by the "dreadful carnage"; he was convinced that it was justified. The Creeks were "Barbarians ignorant of the influence of civilization and government over human powers. . . . The fiends of Tallapoosa will no longer murder our women and children," he told his soldiers. "They have disappeared from the face of the earth." Death so justified held no terror for Andrew Jackson. He had convinced himself long ago that death could bring new order. In the ashes of the Creek encampment he saw renewal: "a new generation will arise who will know their duties better." Jackson believed he had facilitated the rebirth by killing the most important Creek intellectuals, men he believed responsible for instigating the "infernal orgies." When his soldiers found the "famous prophet Monahoee—shot in the mouth by a grape shot," Jackson pronounced it a fitting reward, "as if Heavan designed to chastise his impostures by an appropriate punishment."

"Appropriate punishment": Jackson had these words very much in mind in the following months. His victory at Horse Shoe Bend won him instant national fame, the rank of brigadier general in the U.S. Army, and the command of the entire Gulf region. Delegated to head the final peace negotiations with the Creeks, Jackson was not satisfied with unconditional surrender and a modest indemnity. He wanted to isolate the Creeks forever, to remove them from the way of foreign intrigue, to surround them with white settlers. This would keep "them peacable and faithful." On August 1, 1814, he assembled the remnants of the Creek leadership and forced them to sign away over half of their territory.

As soon as he dictated the Indian treaty, Jackson turned to the defense of the Gulf Coast. Since early spring, the British had been planning an invasion of Louisiana to complement their attack on the east coast. Because they had committed so many troops to the eastern campaign, British strategists accepted the rather optimistic suggestions of Admiral Sir Alexander Cochrane that a force of no more than three thousand men could capture the crucial ports of Mobile and New Orleans. Cochrane counted on massive assistance from the Indians and encouraged recruitment of runaway slaves from Georgia. By mid-summer 1814, his intentions were no longer a secret, although the magnitude and location of the attack remained in doubt. Jackson expected an enormous invasion, believing rumors that 25,000 of Lord Wellington's finest troops had set sail for the Gulf and would be joined by twice that many Russian mercenaries. Jackson immediately began a recruitment campaign of his own, concentrating on the defense of Mobile, where on September 15 his regulars repulsed a British naval force. Much as he relished giving the royal navy such "bloody noses," Jackson was restless. In late October he decided to challenge the new British naval station at Pensacola.

Though only a short distance to the east of Mobile, the city belonged to Spain, and Jackson had been warned not to tread on Spanish neutrality. Jackson knew he was violating orders, but he justified his planned assault on grounds that it would "put an end to the Indian war in the South." His strategy and rationale were popular with his frontier constituency, but the attack, although successful, used valuable time that might have been spent preparing the defense of New Orleans, where Jackson knew the major British attack would come. Fortunately for Andrew Jackson, British offensive plans were no further advanced than his defensive preparations.

Jackson arrived in New Orleans on December 1, 1814, to discover that, despite his numerous written appeals for sacrifice and unification, the populace was hardly prepared for war. The city could muster no more than five hundred soldiers and Jackson had no choice but anxiously to await promised reinforcements. Civil dissension added to the lack of military preparedness. Jackson added to the dissension when he accepted suggestions to arm a unit of free black soldiers. The decision was one of sheer military necessity. As a man, Andrew Jackson had no more respect for free blacks than he had for Indians. As a general, he was willing to employ both in an emergency. He called the blacks to arms in language remark-

ably similar to the paternalistic persuasions of the treaty negotiator. "As Americans, your Country looks with confidence to
her adopted children." Privately he defended his decision on
pragmatic grounds. "They will not remain quiet spectators,"
Jackson told the Louisiana governor. "They will be for, or
against us." Furthermore, Jackson assured anxious authorities
that the blacks would be segregated from white soldiers and
if necessary "moved in the rear to some point where they will
be kept from doing us an injury." Despite these assurances,
the city remained uneasy.

In the ensuing weeks Jackson tried to anticipate the direction of the British attack. Believing New Orleans most vulnerable to a naval expedition up the Mississippi River, he spent
much of his precious time in early December strengthening
the fortifications along the banks of the river. The British,
however, had no intention of braving the navigational hazards
at the mouth of the Mississippi and losing the element of
surprise by running such a lengthy gauntlet. Instead they concentrated their efforts on the northern and eastern water
routes to the city. By using shallow draft vessels they could
move directly from their fleet in the Gulf into Lake Borgne and
from there gain access to numerous bayous that crisscrossed
the fields immediately east of New Orleans. Although Jackson
reconnoitered this area and directed that the bayous be
blocked with fallen trees, he still anticipated a southerly attack.
On December 10, the British navy appeared at the east end of
Lake Borgne; Jackson thought it a feint to draw his attention
from the Mississippi. He still thought so four days later when
Cochrane's forces captured all the American gunboats on the
lake. "With the smiles of heaven I will be able to repulse him,
if he lands, or attempts an invasion up the River." The heavens
smiled by giving Jackson enough time to bring up reinforcements.

Shortly after noon on December 23, the guessing game
ended. A mud-stained messenger burst into Jackson's headquarters with the alarming news that the British army occupied

the levee road, eight miles east of the city. At first, Jackson was incredulous. He had ordered the Louisiana militia to picket all approaches from Lake Borgne and guard the blocked bayous. Had he been in a mood to investigate, Jackson would have discovered the ancient adage that orders issued are not always obeyed. The Bayou Bienvenue, a large channel winding five miles inland from the western reaches of Lake Borgne, was free of obstruction. The British scouts knew this; Jackson did not. In fact, his communications were so feeble that the British were able to land 1,200 men and move them eight miles inland, capturing two militia units in the process. Never one to dwell on his own mistakes, Jackson decided to attack that evening. He realized the hazards of a night battle; his raw recruits might well panic in the dark. Yet he had surprise on his side. If he could keep his men in line, the gamble might pay off. Certainly Jackson was no stranger to a wager. Only a fortnight before he had read in the *Nashville Gazette* that his horse Pacolet had defeated "the noted horse Double-head with great ease." On the night of December 23, Jackson did not win "with great ease," but he did run a dead heat. More important, he upset British plans for quick victory.

Until that evening Cochrane had predicted an easy campaign, boasting that he would have Christmas dinner in New Orleans. The ease of landing and the unchallenged march to the river only heightened British optimism and contempt for the American defenders. Instead of driving directly toward the city, the British troops made camp and promptly built bonfires to ward off the twilight chill. Jackson could see clearly now. Shortly after 8:00 P.M. the American schooner *Carolina* began bombarding the British camp from its anchorage in the Mississippi. This was the signal to attack. For the next four hours the two sides clashed in the smoke and darkness. At midnight the American forces broke off the fight and took up defensive position several miles in front of the British lines. Although he had failed to prevent the enemy from "sleeping on American soil," Jackson had seen to it that Cochrane would have no

Christmas dinner in New Orleans. If the admiral hoped to eat there at all, he would have to bring in more reinforcements.

Having lost the initiative, the British spent nearly two weeks preparing for a frontal assault on Jackson's line. Lord Wellington's brother-in-law, General Sir Edward Pakenham, arrived on Christmas day to assume personal command of the attack. A veteran of the Peninsula campaign against Napoleon, Pakenham was a skillful strategist. But then the cypress swamps of Louisiana bore little resemblance to the plains of Spain. British supply lines stretched nearly sixty miles to the eastern end of Lake Borgne, where the fleet lay at anchor. The British navy had undisputed control of these waters, but Cochrane had failed to order enough shallow-draft supply vessels, making the movement of men and arms a tedious, time-consuming process. Once across the lake, supply trains frequently bogged down in the swampy upper reaches of the Bayou Bienvenue. The only bright spot in this otherwise dismal holiday travail came two days after Christmas when British gunners blew up the *Carolina,* much to Jackson's chagrin.

While Pakenham struggled with these supply problems, Jackson erected a formidable defensive barrier. He set his first line five miles east of the city where the swamp closed to within a thousand yards of the river. Although flat and treeless, the land was intersected by an abandoned mill race running at right angles away from the river, all the way to the swamp. Behind this "canal" Jackson's engineers built a parapet five feet high and in places nearly twenty-five feet thick. Jackson placed his artillery at regular intervals along this wall. By early January his 3,500 men were well entrenched. Since they had withstood several heavy bombardments, he was confident that his forces could hurl back any direct frontal assault.

On January 7, 1815, Jackson received distressing news. The British had cut through the levee and were preparing to cross the Mississippi with the clear intention of attacking the token American force on the opposite banks of the river. Hurriedly, Jackson ordered reinforcements to cover his exposed right flank, but he had no boats and his troops were forced to return to New Orleans, where they had to wait for ferry passage. The delay proved costly.

Pakenham fully intended to exploit this weakness. Under cover of darkness a light brigade was to cross the Mississippi and attack Jackson's batteries before dawn, turning the captured guns on the main American line on the other side of the river. While Jackson coped with this diversion, 1,200 men under General Keane would begin their advance on the right of the main line and 2,200 infantrymen commanded by Major General Gibbs would skirt the swamp and attack the left. The strategy was sound, the execution abominable. Pakenham waited until nightfall on January 7 to move his attack boats from the Villeres canal through the cut in the levee into the Mississippi. At normal water levels, the transfer would have taken but a few hours. The heavens still smiled on Andrew Jackson; that evening the level of the Mississippi fell and with it British hopes for a coordinated attack. It was 3:00 A.M. before the British engineers dragged the last boat through the levee; it was 6:00 A.M. before the light brigade assembled on the other shore. They were still three hours from the American batteries, and the battle had already begun.

In sleep as in death, there is a surrender of consciousness, a resignation to fate. Andrew Jackson slept very soundly before his duel with Charles Dickinson. On the evening of January 7, 1815, he slept very little, arising shortly after midnight to inspect his defenses. He was no stranger to the icy calm before battle, but he had always been the hunter, able to fix the time, the place, even the terms of his encounters with death. Now the British were in control, and Jackson nervously awaited some sign of their attack. Once before he had decided to let his enemy have the first shot and had narrowly escaped with his life. As daylight began to brighten the swirling fog, a British rocket burst above the American line. "That is the signal for advance," Jackson announced. The waiting was over.

A breeze sprang up, clearing away patches of fog, giving the American riflemen their first glimpses of the advancing enemy. The sight was awesome. Two huge red columns massed on the glistening, frost-laden plain, barely six hundred yards away. At a distance, the British looked invincible. Behind the lines all was chaos. Pakenham had lost his shield of darkness and the protective bank of fog was lifting. The attack on the opposite bank could not possibly take place in time. His advance regiment had forgotten to bring its scaling ladders and had sent men scurrying to the rear to retrieve them. He had time to cancel his plans; his formations were still out of range. Instead, Pakenham signaled the advance. This bravery, this foolishness, cost him his life. He did not die alone.

The twin columns advanced and for a time maneuvered precisely. Then the American artillery tore gaping holes in their lines. Still they came. Jackson ordered his cannon to cease fire so that the smoke could clear and the riflemen take aim. Volley after volley exploded across the plain. The red formations wavered under the withering fire. Precision gave way to confusion, confusion to carnage. When the firing stopped two hours later, the white sparkle of frost was still on the ground. The smell of death was everywhere. It lingered well into the next day when a young British officer rode out to help claim the wounded and bury the dead. "Of all the sights I ever witnessed that which met me there was most humiliating. Within the small compass of a few hundred yards were gathered nearly a thousand bodies, all of them arrayed in British uniforms."

The magnitude of the suffering affected even the American defenders. "The slaughter was shocking," John Coffee wrote his wife three weeks after the battle. Jackson was more sanguine and precise. As commander he duly reported the casualties: 300 British dead, including 3 generals and 8 colonels, nearly 1,300 British wounded. He gave his own losses as 6 killed, 7 wounded. Although he reported the figures, Jackson could not comprehend the staggering disproportion. Whereas

Coffee had claimed that on the day of "the grand charge" the Americans had "every advantage we could ask," Jackson was at a loss for strategic explanations. He could only claim divine protection. "The unerring hand of providence shielded my men."

IV

Hero and Victim

RARELY HAVE THE AMERICAN people lavished praise so freely, or with such enthusiasm. To a country weary of war, humiliated by British invasion, weakened by threats of disunion, the news from New Orleans promised salvation. Jackson had lifted the nation "above disgrace." Suddenly American citizens had cause to celebrate. "Glorious," "unparalleled," "incredible"—words almost foreign to the wartime press proclaimed the victory at New Orleans and with it a new era of peace. The mood lingered for several years before giving way to fears of sectional discord and economic chaos, but the magic of New Orleans never faded. It became too much a part of national pride. No matter how confused, how divided, the public could always recall that glorious morning when Jackson repulsed the British charge.

The general was unprepared for fame. Less than eighteen months had elapsed since Jackson set out in search of the Creeks. At Talledega and Horse Shoe Bend he had won recognition from his frontier constituents. At New Orleans, Andrew Jackson captured the attention of the entire nation. Ceremonies celebrating the victory began two weeks after the battle with a special mass of thanksgiving in the cathedral at New Orleans. As Jackson approached the church, young ladies spread flowers in his path and presented him with a laurel wreath.

The public honored the soldier without fully understanding

the man. The American people considered New Orleans a triumph of New World virtue over Old World decadence, a victory of plain farmers over monarchist mercenaries. They wrote of Andrew Jackson's "untutored genius" and cast him as a Cincinnatus, abandoning the plow to take up the sword. The role combined honor with a definite expectation: having conquered the enemy, Jackson and his army would naturally revert to peaceful pursuits.

Jackson had other roles, other generals in mind. Shortly after the battle, a French artist painted him in the manner of Napoleon. Jackson praised the likeness and proudly presented it to one of his close friends. Later that year, when he heard of Napoleon's escape from Elba, Jackson rejoiced: "The *wonderful revolution* in France fills everybody and *nation* with astonishment and the tricoloured cockade being found in the bottom of each soldiers Napsack tells all Urope that Napoleon reigns in the affection of the soldiers." Jackson also basked in the warmth of martial comradeship. He felt at home in the army, enjoyed the company of his staff, and continued to refer to it as his family. Military loyalties weighed heavily in Jackson's subsequent political career. He amply rewarded those who had stood by him in battle, just as he never forgave anyone who brought the slightest discredit to his command.

For Andrew Jackson the War of 1812 was a very personal war. In striking at the nation's enemies, he attempted to conquer his own as well. At New Orleans he was not the feverish adolescent, helplessly surrendering his family to the British and the ravages of war. His body had betrayed him as a youth; as a man his will prevailed. He had endured dysentery in the Creek campaign and, even though wracked by pain, yielded nothing to the British. In the heat of battle, he subdued his agony and fear to concentrate on the enemy a few hundred yards away. He saw them clearly then, just as clearly as he saw his own duty. When they attacked he was ready, firmly in control, able to project his fury with devastating accuracy. "Every Ball and Bomb from our guns carried with them a mission of Death." "Mission," "death"—these were important words to a man who sought to reestablish his right to survive by violent payment of a longstanding family debt. If only the dead could bear witness. "How I wish she could have lived to see this day," he said of his mother shortly after the battle. As the dead can bear no witness, acknowledge no revenge, the survivors are fated to remain prisoners of their own ambivalent emotions. Jackson welcomed fame, even reveled in it, but was fearful that it would pass and even more fearful that someone might deliberately diminish his reputation.

Immediately after the battle of New Orleans, what should have been a period of extended rejoicing turned into a nightmare of spite and intrigue. Continued dysentery no doubt added to Jackson's irascibility. To the dismay of his own officers, the general refused to accept any blame for the British success on the right bank. He charged the Kentucky militia, whom he had ordered to reinforce that position, with cowardice and lack of discipline. Nor did the hero of New Orleans admit any blunder when the British captured Fort Bowyer in early February 1815. Six months previously, this Mobile outpost had been the focal point of Jackson's defenses; it was still under his nominal command at the time of its fall.

The general's anger and stubbornness even soured relations with the people he had saved from British conquest. For nearly two months after the enemy's retreat, Jackson kept New Orleans clamped under martial law. When rumors of peace reached his camp, he refused to relax his vigilance, insisting that until the treaty was actually ratified, the threat of war still existed. Through a series of misunderstandings, he became convinced that the Louisiana legislature had been willing to surrender the city on the eve of the British attack. This conviction, coupled with his low opinion of the governor and his disdain for all legal challenges to his authority, made him an awesome military governor. Peace finally came. Jackson rescinded martial law, but still believed New Orleans harbored a "malicious knot" of "traitors."

The Treaty of Ghent brought an end to the war with England but not to hostilities on the southern frontier. Hard on the heels of Jackson's harsh treaty with the Creeks in 1814 came the march of white settlers, who like the general marveled at the abundance of the land. The cycle began again: Indian retaliation repaid by white revenge, hatred by hatred, massacre by massacre. The treaty that Jackson predicted would place a buffer between red and white society only pushed the conflict closer to the borders of Spanish Florida. Runaway slaves from Georgia used Spanish territory for refuge, forging an informal alliance with the Indians, an alliance that whites had long dreaded. Spain could no more contain these activities than the United States could halt the filibustering expeditions setting forth from its domain. When James Monroe took office in 1817, the Spanish empire was in ruins, making the American acquisition of Florida as certain as the success of the rebellious colonies in Latin America. Like his predecessors, Monroe wanted the acquisition to be peaceful and to be negotiated through diplomatic channels.

The president did not ignore the border upheavals. On December 26, 1817, his new secretary of war, John C. Calhoun, ordered Jackson's subordinate General Edmund P. Gaines to attack the hostile Seminole Indians and, if necessary, follow them into Florida. Although authorized to cross Spain's boundaries, Gaines was under strict instructions not to attack the Indians should they take refuge in a Spanish fort. Gaines was preoccupied with other border troubles; the president decided to turn the mission over to Jackson, who had remained on active service to command the country's new southern military district. There ensued one of the most celebrated and controversial military expeditions in early American history.

In the spring of 1818, in pursuit of the Seminoles, Jackson invaded Spanish territory, captured the towns of St. Marks and Pensacola, put the Spanish governor to flight, and executed two British subjects judged guilty of collaboration with the

Indians. Spanish authorities protested this aggression, placing the Monroe administration in a difficult position. The president did not want to yield the strategic advantage, but he hesitated to endorse Jackson's actions. Clearly the general had violated orders. Yet an official reprimand would be politically embarrassing. Always a man to avoid extremes, Monroe chose the middle course. He relinquished part of Jackson's conquest and privately wrote the general of his displeasure, but he refrained from any official censure. When the shrewd diplomacy of John Quincy Adams led to the final cession of Florida, Monroe appointed Jackson as its first territorial governor.

Although the military and diplomatic aspects of this so-called Seminole affair seem readily comprehensible, the personal and political ramifications became quite involved. Clearly there would have been no affair at all save for the personality of Andrew Jackson. The same urges that drove him into Florida forced him to mount a futile campaign for total vindication.

When he received a copy of Gaines's orders early in January 1818, Jackson was under considerable pressure. The long period of military inactivity made him restless, especially when Indians were disrupting the border areas under his command. His natural inclination was to attack and let the diplomatic chips fall where they might. He had invaded Spanish territory in 1814 and saw nothing wrong with doing so again. A dash across the border would "chastise the ruthless savages" and meet with the "approbation of Heaven." As usual, Jackson believed that he understood frontier realities better than the policy makers in Washington did, but he was reluctant to strike out on his own. He had just concluded an administrative squabble with the War Department that had eventually required the president's intervention. Jackson was flattered by Monroe's support, so much so that he decided not to carry through his oft-repeated threat to resign his commission.

A sense of discrimination was never one of Jackson's virtues. He construed Monroe's blessing quite broadly and indulged it at the first opportunity. On January 6, 1818, he wrote the president suggesting the seizure of East Florida as "an indemnity for the outrages of Spain upon the property of our Citizens." He further proposed that the seizure could be accomplished "without implicating the Government" and suggested that the president transmit his approval through Tennessee's congressman John Rhea. Thus armed, Jackson promised a conquest within "sixty days." Shortly after dispatching this bold overture, he received the formal order to replace Gaines as the head of the expedition. The president never replied to Jackson's letter, nor did he give any assent to the scheme. Apparently he was sick when the message arrived, and he put it aside without reading beyond the first few lines He lived to regret his negligence.

Jackson knew that his seizure of Spanish territory deliberately disobeyed War Department orders. Why else would he write Monroe from Florida that "should my acts meet with your approbation it will be a source of great consolation to me, should it be disapproved, I have this consolation, that I exercised my best exertions and Judgt"? Later in life, when he became an active political candidate, Jackson perceived the weakness of his position and maintained that Monroe had indeed given his blessing through Rhea, that Rhea had communicated them to him, and that Jackson had destroyed the letter at Monroe's request. This explanation lay more than a decade in the future and reveals more about Jackson's presidential personality than about his motives in 1818.

In that fateful spring Jackson seemed bent on recapturing his moment of military triumph, fearful lest death interrupt. He spoke often of his ailments, once reporting to Monroe that "fatigue and a bad cough with a pain in my left side which produced a spitting of blood, has reduced me to a skeleton. It is uncertain whether my constitution can be restored to stand the fatigue of another campaign." If this was to be his last military command, Jackson wanted to achieve some tangible national goals. In the Creek war and at New Orleans, he had defended American property. In Florida, he conquered, proudly hoisting "the American Eagle over the Ramparts of Ft. don Carlos de Barancas and Pensacola." Having done so, he advised the president that "sound national policy will dictate holding possession as long as we are a republick," which is how long Jackson hoped his own fame would endure.

Jackson was hardly prepared for the political onslaught that followed his invasion and took the partisan criticism as personal insult. Alarmed at the general's growing popularity, a number of presidential aspirants used the congressional investigating procedure in an attempt to condemn the seizure of Spanish territory. As predicted by Jackson's supporters, the congressional censure failed, but not before the general had stormed around the city, issuing challenges and allegedly threatening to cut the ears off a member of the Senate investigating committee. Although friends prevented Jackson from making a public spectacle of himself, they never calmed his anger or allayed his suspicions. These emotions would have a direct bearing on Jackson's involvement in Indian affairs.

That the general whose armies brought devastation to the borderlands of the Southwest should be designated as diplomat and negotiator is one of the tragic ironies of the period following the peace of 1815. Andrew Jackson dominated this crucial period of Indian diplomacy, a period that determined the fate of the five "civilized tribes." He personally presided at more than half of the major treaty negotiations during the Monroe administrations. When not present, he often exercised great inflence through the commissioners, many of whom were his friends or former military comrades.

By the time Jackson went to the treaty grounds, the nation was already debating whether to move the Indians west of the Mississippi. President Thomas Jefferson had thought portions of the Louisiana purchase might make a suitable Indian home. His successors tried to convince the tribes to cede eastern land for territory in the west. Simultaneously, the federal government supported missionary programs to "civilize" eastern tribesmen in the hope that by adopting white customs, Indians could integrate into white society. In many instances, this program succeeded to the point of embarrassment. The Cherokees, for instance, developed a high degree of literacy, learned English as a second language, and even published a newspaper. Such dramatic changes in tribal culture, coupled with the growth of an extensive Indian plantation network throughout the Southwest, contradicted the age-old argument that the Indian was a nomadic savage, incapable of building a peaceful, agrarian social order. Furthermore, a number of "mixed bloods" and "half breeds" who had adopted white ways rose to positions of leadership in their tribes; instead of encouraging removal, they advocated retention and development of the ancient tribal lands.

Contradictions always bothered Andrew Jackson, who prized order as much as he valued control. He found the government's Indian policy devoid of both. He objected primarily to the historic practice of treating Indian tribes as foreign nations. Calling the arrangement an "absurdity," Jackson argued that "Indians are subjects of the United States" and urged that they be brought under congressional control. Although paying lip service to the idea of civilization, the intent of Jackson's policy was to destroy tribal structure, replacing it with the "fostering care" of the central government, which would then "prescribe their bounds at will." Without such control, the "real Indians, the natives of the forest" would fall prey to the "designing half breeds and renegade white men who have taken refuge in their country." "For it is too true," he believed, "that avarice and fear are the predominant passions that govern an Indian."

Similar feelings guided Jackson's policies as a treaty negotiator. He urged the government to bring ceded Indian lands "into the market" and have them "populated." Only white settlement could bring adequate defense to an area that "for thirty years" had been the "den of murderers." In 1816, Jackson succeeded in having his former cavalry commander, John Coffee, appointed to survey conquered Creek lands and settle the conflicting claims that arose following the war. Like so many colonial surveyors before him, Coffee turned public service to private profit, becoming one of the largest land owners and speculators in Alabama. The names of Overton, Donelson, and Lewis also appeared in the land registers. For himself, Jackson claimed very little; he bought a small estate for his ward, Andrew J. Hutchings, but the plantation never proved particularly profitable and Jackson sold it within a decade. He realized more from the sale of Indian lands in western Tennessee, but by comparison with the huge land grabs of the day, Jackson's own speculations were modest. Nevertheless, the general's negotiations served the wealthy speculators, as the profits of his friends clearly reveal.

Avarice did not shape Jackson's policies nearly so much as did his fear of disorder. It was an old fear, one that had haunted him since adolescence, one given harrowing dimension by the Indian attacks and resulting social instability in the Cumberland. Military authority enabled him to conquer that fear by striking at the root of disorder. In quick succession, he had destroyed the "murderers," seized their territory, and prescribed limits to future Indian aggression. He did not sicken at the carnage nor quaver at the awful finality of death. He felt justified in destroying those who threatened society, and he believed that their death would bring a new social order in which white and Indian could coexist. By surrounding the Indians with "an industrious and virtuous population you set them good examples, their manners habits and customs will be imbibed and adopted."

The same coercive paternalism governed his treatment of the Indian child Lyncoya. Jackson had great ambitions for his Creek ward, all of which denied the boy's cultural heritage. Jackson wanted Lyncoya to learn English, adopt white ways, and eventually attend West Point. Lyncoya proved a disappointment to his benefactor; the child's "racial tendancies began to appear." He took to smearing his face with paint, hiding behind bushes, and frightening local children. Death removed Lyncoya from his foster home shortly before his guardian removed the Creeks from their ancient domain.

In 1821 Jackson decided to resign from the army to become the first territorial governor of Florida, a decision both he and President Monroe came to regret. Jackson regarded the appointment as further vindication of his conduct in the Seminole affair and set out to organize the new territory with military efficiency. By placing his own friends in positions of influence, he hoped to attract to the area "a respectable population" that could permanently defend the nation's borders. Privately, he told relatives that "a great field is now open to the real capitalist, and real property well situated must in a few years become very valuable." In essence, Jackson intended to govern Florida as he had settled Indian affairs, by using private patronage to advance the cause of frontier defense and security.

The blunt tactics that had made him master of the treaty grounds disrupted civil governance. Within weeks after the formal transfer of Florida, Jackson violated diplomatic traditions by throwing the former Spanish governor in jail after a dispute over legal documents and by defying a writ of habeas corpus issued by Florida's new federal judge. Spanish authorities in Washington protested the arrest, opposition newspapers took up the cry, and soon Monroe found himself in the distasteful but all-too-familiar position of trying to explain Jackson's behavior to irate members of Congress. By the time the president delivered his carefully reasoned defense in December 1821, Jackson had already resigned, claiming fatigue and ill health. Deeply disturbed by the congressional outcry, Jackson blamed his predicament on yet another conspiracy. This time he believed that his tormentors had been particularly ingenious: knowing the impossible administrative problems in Florida, they had deliberately secured his appointment so that he might disgrace himself.

spite the congressional furor, Jackson retained his public
larity. The Florida interlude in no way tarnished his mili-
reputation, nor did it disappoint admirers of his Indian
tiations. Yet by 1821, the United States had more need
olitical cohesion than for martial authority. A people who
boasted of Jackson's heroism suddenly found themselves
by the disruptive forces of social and economic change.
Neither the choruses of unbridled nationalism nor the echoes
of self-congratulation could drown out the rumblings of dismay. Americans felt threatened, not by want or anarchy, but
by the forces of progress.

The crude eighteenth-century wagon roads that had carried
the Jacksons to the back country and bore their offspring to the
Cumberland gave way to turnpikes and the turnpikes to canals.
Eventually the canals would give way to railroads. With each
progression, public enthusiasm swelled, until the coffers of
private and state finance strained to the breaking point. Transportation companies might fail, banks close, legislatures
plunge into debt, but the passion endured, fed by the realiza-
tion that the Republic had developed the means to conquer a
continent. Although it affected the entire nation, the transportation revolution was disjointed, haphazard, and uncontrolled.
For a brief period after the War of 1812, the country united
through its legislature and embarked on a campaign of federal
projects, like the National Road stretching west from Cumberland, Maryland. By the time this grand highway had reached
the Ohio in 1818, congressional unanimity was floundering on
the rocks of sectional jealousy. New York would build its great
canal, but not with the aid of the central government. By the
time the canal reached Buffalo in 1825, national projects had
become objects of derision, their sponsors targets of political
assault. The transportation craze continued, lodged in the
individual state and private corporations that made the spirit
of competition synonymous with the American character.
With roads and canals crossing nature's barriers, the restless

Americans began to move. Jackson's Indian conquests opened up huge tracts of fertile land in the deep South, land that would soon give rise to an entrenched cotton culture and slavery. Tidewater planters fretted about the loss of population; they were unable to stop the flow. New Englanders voiced similar concerns about the massive migrations that left towns deserted, pulpits vacant. They, too, were powerless. Cities grew and multiplied, threatening comfortable, agrarian self-images. Immigrants began to arrive in ever-increasing numbers, some joining in the journey west, others contributing to the burgeoning urban population.

With the first faint rumblings of expansion, people began to search for remedies to ease their discomfort. Religious revivals renewed faith and suggested new mechanisms for acting on general concerns. Missionary societies flourished in the first quarter of the nineteenth century, offering the distraught faithful an opportunity to ennoble themselves at home by supporting God's work abroad. By the time the first missions were firmly established in the Sandwich Islands, a host of reform societies had sprung up, each trying to cope with the symptoms of national unrest. Convert the heathen, institutionalize the insane, remove the Indians, protect the Sabbath, reform the drunkard, deport the blacks: through these crusades, Americans sought to regain control over their society. Like the forces of change, these institutional remedies were frenzied and uncoordinated. All this activity took place in an atmosphere of intense introspection; old heroes were summoned to pass on reassurances that the nation was not deserting its revolutionary heritage.

The heroes appeared and bestowed their blessings, but some, like Thomas Jefferson, mixed blessing with warning. The nation was dividing over the crucial issue of slavery. Division lay in the future, but concern grew daily. Political stratagems like the Missouri Compromise sufficed for a time, but the nation's political institutions were too frail, too decentralized, too disjointed to provide permanent solutions.

This weakness was particularly evident in the nation's capital. Despite its architectural pretensions, Washington was an isolated community that never quite realized the classical illusions of its creators. The original design attempted to preserve in spatial relation what the founding fathers had set down in the constitution—that special separation of powers considered essential to liberty and freedom. By the early 1820s the community was deeply separated, more by political ambition than constitutional theory. "Mr. Monroe is reelected unanimously," reported one senator, yet "the measures of the govt. are without friends in Congress."

Like the city he ruled, the president was isolated, a victim of public apathy and political factionalism. In a sense, the chief executive derived his strength from the legislature, having been nominated by his party's congressional caucus. He had to cultivate good relations with Congress. The nation's primitive communications network denied him any direct appeal for popular support, and members of his own official family had divided loyalties. So long as the cabinet was a stepping-stone to the executive mansion, its members courted the political brokers on Capitol Hill. To maintain control of the legislature, the president had to maintain discipline. By 1820, "Mr. Monroe's party" had been in power for two decades and had fallen prey to its own success. No sooner had they vanquished the Federalist opposition than Republicans began quarreling among themselves. The president faced the nearly impossible task of trying to manage a group of bickering legislators whose very conception of their office valued independence more than discipline.

In the twilight of the Virginia dynasty even the congressional brokers seemed out of step with the times. Totally preoccupied by the intrigues for succession to the presidency, they remained insensitive to the rapid economic and social changes that buffeted state politics. With roads to build, canals to dig, banks to charter, Indians to control, and land to develop, statehouses became political battlegrounds. The spoils of war mounted with each passing session. Old methods of management suddenly seemed obsolete. There were too many new voters, too many insistent cries for state action. A new breed of politician arose to meet this challenge, men for whom politics became vocation not avocation, for whom discipline was more important than deference, for whom the interests of the states took priority over those of the national government.

Martin Van Buren was such a man. He reached political maturity amid the economic enthusiasm that swept New York after the War of 1812. An avowed enemy of the state's popular governor, De Witt Clinton, Van Buren and his fellow "Bucktails" created an efficient, well-disciplined organization that wrested the legislature from Clinton's grasp in 1820. Control of the legislative machinery conveyed enormous benefits, especially with the Erie Canal nearing completion, the western reaches of the state falling open to development, and 16,000 patronage positions to distribute.

Having established this strong economic base and extensive patronage system, the Albany Regency went in search of national political power. As a newly elected Republican senator, Van Buren left for Washington in 1821, fully expecting the Monroe administration to repay his loyal support. He soon discovered that the terms discipline and loyalty had never been included in the lexicon of Republican politics. The president practiced a policy of "amalgamation," inviting former Federalists to return to political life under Republican auspices. Disgusted, Van Buren joined the growing ranks of the disaffected, vowing to work toward a "general resuscitation of the old democratic party."

Steeped in Jeffersonian dogma, Van Buren hoped to adapt the twin theories of state rights and limited government to the realities of an era of expansion. He knew that no coalition could succeed without some basic mechanism for resolving the sectional tensions that emerged following the Missouri debates of 1820. In addition to encouraging local activism, the doctrine of state rights promised protection for such promi-

nent local institutions as slavery, and it was therefore emi-
nently practical as the theoretical framework for an in-
tersectional alliance. The South was gradually losing its control over national politics; Van Buren believed that by backing
a Southern candidate for president, he could help renew the
once powerful New York–Virginia alliance. In 1824 he committed the Regency to support Georgia's William H. Crawford, whose state-rights sympathies had already won approval
from Virginia's leading strategists. Although Crawford could
legitimately lay claim to the Jeffersonian mantle, he was far too
wedded to the power structure of the Washington community;
he epitomized the very system that Van Buren and other insur-
gents were trying to reform.

Andrew Jackson soon found himself in the thick of these
maneuvers, although like many of his contemporaries he never
fully understood the economic and social forces that were so
drastically altering American political life. As early as 1816,
friends mentioned him as a possible presidential candidate.
Jackson greeted such suggestions with uncharacteristic modesty. "Do they think I am such a damned fool!" he snorted.
"No sir, I know what I am fit for. I can command a body of men
in a rough way; but I am not fit to be President." In all proba-
bility, Jackson was afraid to risk his newly acquired reputation
by submitting it to the intense scrutiny of a political campaign.
In 1816 Jackson considered himself a military man. "Political
discussion," he once lectured Crawford, "is not the province
of a military officer."

In Jackson's view, political parties were evil because they
encouraged the "lowest kind of intrigue" with the sole purpose of allowing "those in power to aggrandize themselves."
Like so many of his countrymen, Jackson believed that the
country would be far better off without organized parties.
"Now is the time to put them down," he urged the president-
elect in 1816. The administration could begin by selecting a
former Federalist as secretary of war. Party labels were "but
Bubbles"; they did not measure an individual's character;

there were Federalists and there were Federalists. Those who had preached disunion and had organized the Hartford convention in 1814 Jackson would have "hung up." "These kind of men altho called Federalist are really monarchist and traitors." Among the rest were individuals of honesty and virtue, who might "differ in many respects and opinions with the republicans" but who would support the government and "risque everything in its defense."

Jackson conceived of party discipline as he conceived of military discipline—in terms of personal loyalty. He welcomed former Federalists as he welcomed Indian allies, with little respect for their "opinions" and with considerable doubts about their intentions. Despite public acclaim, Jackson retained something of an orphan's distrust of overtures of friendship. "Have apparent confidence in all," he advised one young military protégé, "but never make a confidant of any until you have proven him worthy of it." For Jackson the proof of worthiness was always personal loyalty, never political principle or ideological persuasion. Because of these suspicions, Jackson never fully understood the concept of a party based on issues. Nor did he ever accept the possibility of a legitimate political opposition. Criticism, however dispassionate, was a personal insult.

As Jackson's laurels withered under the heat of repeated congressional investigation, he became more convinced that the political system was hopelessly corrupt and opened himself to suggestions that his election to the presidency might bring reform. There was no false modesty now. "If elevated to the presidential chair by the free will of the people," he wrote after resigning from the army, he would go "there with clean hands, without bargain, pledge, or management. ..." The fiasco in Florida only increased this sense of outraged dignity. Despite his oft-repeated wishes for the solitude of his plantation, retirement proved agonizing. Neither political foes nor physical complaints would grant him peace. "I must take rest or my stay here on earth cannot be long." Tennessee politicians soon took advantage of Jackson's apocalyptic anxieties.

Fame had been fickle. Feted, honored, and acclaimed throughout the nation, Andrew Jackson was cordially hated by a substantial number of prominent Tennessee leaders. Part of this hatred resulted from his long association with the Blount faction, part from his violent quarrels and disputes, the rest from sheer envy. All the enmity was politically damaging. Convinced that electioneering was demeaning, Jackson had made little attempt to improve his standing within the state, relying instead on the traditional appeal of his army affiliations. When the Panic of 1819 created widespread cries for debtor relief and fiscal reform, other members of the ruling elite responded, but not Jackson. To his dismay, his former military compatriot William Carroll, whose well-placed bullet had found Jesse Benton's posterior, used the relief question to win election as governor of Tennessee in 1821, thereby establishing a dominance over the state's politics that would last for more than a decade.

Carroll's enemies wanted to challenge this dominance by defeating the governor's candidate for the United States Senate in 1823, John Williams. Willing to toy with Jackson's emotions to do so, they cynically calculated that even though the Old Hero could not possibly be elected, his nomination for president by the Tennessee legislature would attract widespread attention and redound to their advantage in the senatorial election. They convinced Jackson by appealing to his wounded pride, telling him that a presidential nomination would disprove all the national rumors that "you are not popular at home."

This native son candidacy failed to halt the Carroll forces. When Williams seemed on the verge of victory, Jackson's friends rushed their presidential hopeful into the senatorial lists. The Tennessee legislature selected Jackson for the United States Senate by a narrow margin of 35 to 25. With some reluctance, Jackson bowed to "the will of the majority"; he agreed to forgo "private ease" for public service. Behind the mask of *noblesse oblige* lay intense inner turmoil. He hated to leave Rachel once again, but most of all he was dismayed at the behavior of the opposition. Why did they not withdraw once his name was submitted? Why did they oppose him to the bitter end? "Corruption" and "intrigue" were his only answers. In this agitated frame of mind, Jackson returned to Nashville; enroute "i was taken with a palpitation of heart with great fluttering, I rode . . . 23 miles, it continued with occasional blindness."

If Old Hickory was temporarily blinded, his political managers certainly were not. What had started as a strategy for local advantage soon blossomed into a campaign of surprising national strength. Jackson had come forward at precisely the right time. The congressional nominating machinery was falling apart, having been badly damaged by the conflicting aspirations of four prominent Washington figures: Secretary of War John C. Calhoun, Secretary of State John Quincy Adams, Secretary of the Treasury William H. Crawford, and House Speaker Henry Clay. Popular disapproval completed what excessive ambition had begun; to a citizenry increasingly attracted by democratic rhetoric, the caucus became a symbol of vested interests and aristocracy. With the central party structure in disarray, local newspapers and state legislatures made their own evaluations of a candidate's fitness. All this was to Jackson's advantage. To the South he was slaveholder; to the Scotch Irish of Pennsylvania he was kin; to the frontiersmen of the Southwest he was protector; to former Federalists he was forgiving spoilsman; to all he was military hero.

Jackson benefited by the collapse of men as well as machinery. After the general's impressive showing in Pennsylvania's nominating convention of 1823, Calhoun withdrew. A stroke nearly cost Crawford his life. He remained in seclusion in his Georgia home, his health shattered, his strength ebbing, his forces leaderless. As senator, Jackson tried to seclude himself but for different reasons. He was determined to stand "entirely aloof from the intriguers and caucus mongers" in

Washington, fearing that his reputation might be contaminated by this "unclean procedure." He would "become the perfect philosopher" and disappoint those "whose minds were prepared to see me with a Tomahawk in one hand, and a scalping knife in the other." Jackson disclaimed any real desire to be president but looked forward to the election nevertheless. By displaying himself as a civilized, austere, and dignified gentleman, he would put down the slanders once and for all. The candidate desperately wanted such vindication. "I court it from the nation."

Jackson's habitual insecurity and jaundiced view of politics help explain this posture. Since his adolescent encounter with death, he had felt vulnerable to attack. When threatened, he responded by flying into destructive rage or by wrapping himself in a cloak of injured innocence, claiming that his pursuers were evil, that he was pure, and that providence would attest to both. Mission and rage—sometimes singly, often in unison —protected him against the fear of death. Because of the turmoil of his military career, Jackson considered the Washington community the haven of his enemies. Twice he had endured congressional investigations of his conduct, investigations that challenged not just his judgment but his character. Although exonerated on both occasions, Jackson never forgave his inquisitors or accepted their inquisitions as normal partisan activity. In Jackson's view, politics was evil, its practitioners corrupt, their ambitions venal, and their motives conspiratorial. Tormenting though these thoughts were, they provided some comfort. Convinced that his critics were immoral, Jackson never had to worry that their charges were true and felt fully justified in trying to silence their slanders.

Jackson never admitted political ambition, for it was the source of intrigue, the main sin of men like Crawford whom Jackson privately called "The Great Whore of Babylon." "Intrigue may stalk around me," Jackson claimed, "but it cannot move me from my purpose." No, he wanted to be president, not to acquire power for its own sake, but to bring reform. By winning the election, he could crush the corrupt caucus and prove that honesty not intrigue should rule the nation's affairs. Jackson took little joy in this mission: "to be a slave to office for my declining years has no charms for me," he said. Yet he saw no alternative. Duty called and he was "prepared to say the Lord's will be done, and if I should be brought into the presidential chair, imploring the benediction of heavan, I will endeavour to administer it for the good of the nation regardless of any other consideration."

The people shared Jackson's sense of injury and resented the secrecy shrouding the caucus. They naturally sympathized with a man who had no ties to such a closed, elitist system, a man whose fame rested upon martial feats, not partisan maneuvers. Given widespread public discontent, even Jackson's tiffs with congressional committees became political assets. They proved his determination not to submit to the cabal, just as many voters refused to bend to the political dictates of the caucus. In the fall balloting in 1824, Jackson received nearly a third more popular votes than John Quincy Adams and triple the totals of Crawford and Clay. Still, Old Hickory lacked a majority of the electoral votes, and the contest was thrown into the House of Representatives.

Disappointed, Jackson vowed to remain aloof in the months ahead. He made little attempt to influence the outcome in the House. To have done so would have been to dabble in intrigue. "I will not, have not, in the least interfered," Jackson claimed a month before the House vote. "I would feel myself degraded to be placed in that office but by the free and unsolicited voice of the people." But of course the people had no voice in the House of Representatives. Only the politicians could speak with conviction and Jackson was not listening to them, nor bargaining with them either. By becoming the "perfect philosopher" he lost all hope of becoming president.

Even had he authorized overtures to Clay and Crawford, it is doubtful that Jackson could have won their support. Crawford was clinging to the hope of a congressional deadlock as

tenaciously as he was clinging to life itself. Although elimi-
nated from contention, Clay had little reason to make Jackson
the first Western president; he wanted to reserve that distinc-
tion for himself. Nor was Jackson's small band of partisans
experienced at congressional maneuvering. They stood helplessly by when Clay announced his support for Adams a month
before the voting. They seemed just as helpless when on February 9, 1825, the House elected the New Englander on the
first ballot. In the wake of defeat, Jackson's manager, Senator
John Eaton, had cause to remember his stern preelection
warning that the general's friends needed to "do something
more than *pray for him.*"

Jackson was hardly philosophical in defeat. He came to the
House vote armed with a rationalization: only corruption
could thwart the people's will. "If party or intrigue should
prevail and exclude me, I shall retire to my comfortable farm
with great pleasure." This studied indifference vanished once
the ballots were counted. "Demagogues barter them as
sheep," Jackson said of the voters the day after Adams's triumph. Then came a Godsend! In a move he would later publicly regret, Henry Clay accepted the president-elect's offer to
become secretary of state, confirming Jackson's worst suspicions and providing ample grist for the campaign mill. "The
Judas of the west has closed the contract," the enraged general
repeated again and again as if in secret delight. "Our government rests upon virtue . . . and unless repaired by the virtue
of the people, the fair fabric . . . must tumble." Rage, revenge,
mission: the cycle began again; Jackson would "retire" to his
"comfortable farm," not "with great pleasure," but with firm
determination to seek redress in the next presidential canvass.
For the next four years, he prepared himself for that ordeal.

To the public, Andrew Jackson was now both hero and
victim. Clay's appointment seemed to confirm what Jackson's
supporters had long been saying: corruption dominated the
highest levels of government. This sense of outrage coincided

with broader concerns for the nation's well-being. Unprecedented westward migration, a large influx of immigrants, economic boom, financial collapse, slave expansion, and slave rebellion upset the rhythm of American life. State politicians reacted as best they could, devising programs to settle new land, regulate financial growth, guard against failure, and protect the institution of slavery. Although they expected little in the way of national legislation, these leaders hoped the central government would not frustrate their efforts to achieve stability. Instead, the intrigues of the Washington community increased the confusion, as did President Adams, who proposed an ambitious program of public works that seemed destined to heighten interstate rivalry and further sectional discord.

Jackson promised relief, not by legislative act or executive program, but by removing the major source of decay: governmental corruption. He vowed to slay King Caucus, remove its proponents, and end its hold over the central government. Troubled and dismayed, eager and ambitious, the people responded to this appeal by renewed support for the state organizations that were mobilizing to carry forward the Jackson crusade. Fervor and spirit the new alliance had; structure and sophistication it lacked.

The Jacksonian alliance was not a unified national party, not by modern definition at least. Some state organizations did find new ways to appeal to a burgeoning electorate and in the process anticipated some modern electoral techniques. Certainly the Albany Regency embodied a new spirit of professionalism; still, Van Buren was not undisputed master of the Empire state. He could not deliver all New York's electoral votes. Van Buren negotiated his cherished alliance with the Old Dominion on the basis of state-rights ideology, not on a shared appreciation for political method. The Richmond Junto, as the Virginia leadership came to be known, bore little resemblance to its New York counterpart. Instead of discipline, the Junto continued to honor deference, a staple com-

modity in Virginia politics since the eighteenth century. John
C. Calhoun's power in South Carolina rested on an even more
reactionary, antidemocratic regime.

Jackson's own Nashville Junto was but a small coterie of
devoted friends led by his longtime associate John Overton. A
short, angular, "queer looking little old man," Overton had
"lost his teeth" and consequently tended to "swallow his lips."
The loss mattered little as neither he nor his colleagues John
Eaton, Alfred Balch, Sam Houston, and William B. Lewis had
to make public speeches. Instead their duties consisted of
defending their candidate against the charges arising during
the campaign. Known as the whitewash committee, this group
churned out innumerable documents attesting to Jackson's
virtue and circulated them throughout the states. Although
Eaton and Overton enjoyed some prominence in Tennessee
politics, the Nashville Junto was primarily an electoral organization with little power in the state legislature. Jackson
would always be embarrassed that Tennessee honored him in
presidential elections but rejected his friends for state office.

Nor did Jackson's new national organization have teeth.
Joining with other presidential critics, his congressional supporters helped elect Virginia's Andrew Stevenson as Speaker
of the House of Representatives in December 1827. The victory weakened Adams's control over House committees but
did not signal the emergence of a disciplined, Jacksonian congressional corps. Even a staunch partisan like James K. Polk
admitted that to elect Stevenson "we had to fight some undisciplined militia against well-drilled regulars." Drill though
they might, there was little way for Jackson's floor managers
to overcome the congressmen's traditional antipower bias and
their aversion to regularity, now highlighted by Jackson's own
public denunciations of management and intrigue. A small
group of Jackson's followers did oversee distribution of committee reports adverse to Adams's cause, but this was not a
startling innovation, merely politics as usual.

The country's primitive communications system posed the

greatest obstacle to development of national party machinery. Newspapers flourished throughout the states, but none had a circulation in excess of a few thousand copies. The precursors of the large-circulation, low-cost journal would not arrive for nearly a decade and would then appear primarily in metropolitan areas. National news consisted of the printed debates of Congress, partisan editorials, plus tidbits of Washington gossip, all arriving weeks after the fact because of slow mail delivery. Readers saw little reason to patronize a national newspaper when events at the capital would eventually appear in their own journals, along with outdated information from other "foreign" cities such as London, Paris, Boston, and Philadelphia.

Jackson's strategists tried to establish a strong newspaper in Washington under the editorship of Duff Green. In 1826, Green secured nearly $1,500 from the Nashville Junto to finance the *United States Telegraph;* subsequent loans and even a congressional printing contract failed to ease Green's financial burden. His plight was not unusual. Even Thomas Ritchie, spokesman for the Richmond Junto and proprietor of the *Richmond Enquirer,* moaned about the impossible demands of partisan journalism. "If you have a thousand sons," he advised a prominent Virginia Democrat, "don't bring one up to be an editor." Although Jackson convinced a number of the nation's editors to adopt his cause, they remained dependent on their subscribers and patrons for financial support.

The entire Jackson coalition depended upon the ability of autonomous state organizations to "forget their minor differences," as one optimistic Democratic strategist put it, "and unite in one great common defence." "Defence" aptly characterizes the negative nature of the Jacksonian campaign; opposition to the administration of John Quincy Adams bound these state organizations together. Jackson rarely issued statements on national issues. When he did, his arguments were extremely vague, leaving local politicians ample leeway to interpret his beliefs as they thought best. "If he is elected *every interest* of the *nation* will be attended to," read one typical assurance from Jackson's main correspondence committee.

Van Buren, Ritchie, and other prominent state-rights advocates had more concrete expectations. They hoped that Jackson would pledge himself to a strict construction of the Constitution, to a limit on the power of the federal government, thereby eliminating any restraints on the state activism that had brought renewed vigor to the nation's politics. Van Buren considered Jeffersonian ideas essential to the maintenance of the emerging anti-Adams alliance. Without such ideological commitment the new party might tear itself apart, giving rise to the forces of sectionalism "or what is worse, prejudice between the free and slaveholding states." Although Jackson publicly acknowledged the primacy of Jeffersonian principles, Van Buren remained uneasy, fearing that the election would be "the result of his military service without reference to party."

Such fears were not without foundation. Voters might wonder where Andrew Jackson stood on the tariff and internal improvements, but they were never allowed to forget his stand at New Orleans. A new inexpensive edition of his campaign biography appeared; begun by a former military aide and completed by John Eaton, the book extolled Jackson's battlefield exploits. To help rekindle the martial spirit, Old Hickory returned to New Orleans in January 1828, on the pretext of attending a nonpartisan celebration of the thirteenth anniversary of the British defeat. Despite an overwhelming display of popular enthusiasm, Jackson felt uncomfortable in his new role as soldier turned democratic spokesman. At one point in the trip down river, he grabbed a rifle and threatened to shoot a steamboat captain who was maneuvering his vessel for a glimpse of the Old Hero. After the ceremonies in New Orleans, Jackson retreated from public view to the seclusion of the Hermitage. Here he remained through the final months of the campaign, isolated from the people as tradition required.

John Eaton and other party members hoped to isolate the

candidate's legendary temper as well. During the campaign of 1828, a campaign in which both sides disgraced themselves by their slanders, Jackson felt called upon to defend both his private and public reputation. Scurrilous newspaper stories attacked the legitimacy of his marriage and even charged his "pious mother, nearly fifty years in the tomb" with being "a prostitute who intermarried with a negro." Jackson exploded, his rage tinged with racial and sexual doubts that he projected on his opponents. He wanted desperately to attack them openly. "It is time to carry the *war* into *africa,*" he vowed; to close the congressional "*sewers* through which the vile slanders against Mrs. Jackson has been circulated ... by prostituting the franking privelege." Still, Jackson's managers dissuaded him from rushing into print. "I know it is goading in the extreme to see falsehoods and shafts flying in all directions," Eaton told Jackson's close friend John Coffee. "Nevertheless the General should be patient, & above all silent—silent." A personal statement, his managers argued, would only detract from the carefully drawn portrait of a Cincinnatus "in retirement on your farm, calm and unmoved by the excitement around you."

Uncomfortable though it was, Jackson played the role of Cincinnatus and played it well. His state supporters promised the electorate a return to simple government, presided over by a benevolent hero who had agreed to leave the retirement of his agrarian retreat to combat the forces of corruption. By avoiding any discussion of how Jackson might wage this war, by stressing instead his advanced age and political innocence, Democratic strategists neatly sidestepped the inherent dilemma in Old Hickory's candidacy: How could a president serve the cause of reform and limited government at the same time?

The voters were too preoccupied to worry about this dilemma. Upset by social, economic, and political change, a substantial segment of the American electorate applauded the promise of an end to corruption and a return to the "Arcadian past." In celebrating the miracle of New Orleans, the voters recalled more than military heroism; they remembered the order that it had preserved. In the fall of 1828 Jackson received nearly 56 percent of the popular vote, registering strength in all areas of the country save Adams's stronghold of New England.

By itself, the election constituted neither electoral nor political revolution. King Caucus was dead, yet the demise came more at the hands of political brokers than of outraged citizens. To replace the caucus, these regicides adopted the state and national convention system. Van Buren maintained that such reform was "in union" with the democratic sentiments of the age; the Red Fox was a realist. He was confident that Jackson's supporters could use the convention, as politicians had used the caucus, to promote party discipline rather than to increase popular participation in the electoral process. To Van Buren's dismay, the convention proved as inefficient as it was elitist. The Jacksonian Democrats would not hold their first national convention until 1832; then they would fail to win unanimous party endorsement for a national ticket. Nor did the election of 1828 feature a dramatic rush to the national polls. Americans continued to vote more heavily in state than in national elections.

Although his election was no political revolution, Jackson's campaign contained the seeds of modern electoral practices. Relaxation of suffrage requirements had increased the number of eligible voters, just as the growing concern over social and economic problems stimulated public interest in politics, especially at the state level. Jackson strategists responded to these stimuli as best they could, fashioning a loose coalition of state organizations. Thus constructed, the Jackson party could not promise a broad program of legislative redress; the central government was too weak to control the forces of expansion, and state political interests were too insistent on retaining power. Rather, the party coalesced around a man whose heroism was non-partisan and did not threaten state interests, and whose campaign avoided specific programs but pledged that the days of secrecy, intrigue, and undemocratic management were over. In celebration of that heroism, party leaders staged rallies, barbecues, and demonstrations that set the tone for national elections to come.

Jackson's adherents rejoiced at the election results, but some feared he might carry the crusade too far and forget the party's pledge to limit the power of the central government. "I hope the General will not find it necessary," Van Buren fretted before the inauguration, "to avow any opinions upon the constitutional questions at war with the doctrines of the Jefferson school." Jackson was at war, not with political doctrine, but with an unprincipled enemy whom he blamed for the slander that clouded his triumph and frustrated his search for vindication.

V

President
and Defender

ANDREW JACKSON groped for the right words to explain his ambivalent feelings about the election results. "I am filled with gratitude, still my mind is depressed," he said shortly after receiving formal notification of his victory. At no time in the months ahead did he speak of party triumph or political mandate. His thoughts were intensely self-centered and almost entirely concerned with corruption and providential retribution. Thanks to "the great ruler of the universe" he had survived "the most bitter and wicked persecution, recorded in history." Jackson fully appreciated "the suffrages of a virtuous people," not because they anticipated a new era of politics, but because he felt they "pronounced a verdict of condemnation" against the "corrupt minions of a profligate administration" and "justified my character and course." How the candidate must have yearned to defend his character personally, instead of entrusting it to the care of his managers. Unable to speak out, Jackson was unable to find relief. With the luxury of time and further reflection, the president-elect might have taken a broader, less conspiratorial view of the election. But the "providence" that snatched him "from the snares of the fowler" suddenly plunged him into the dark abyss. On December 22, 1828, his wife died of a heart attack.

For weeks the distraught husband was immobilized; grief

and guilt overwhelmed him. He knew that Rachel had been ill, that his constant absences had contributed to her growing despondency. Yet he could no more abandon his search for public vindication than she could cast aside her role as dutiful helpmate. They were prisoners of the ambition and social convention that troubled their last years together at the Hermitage. Throughout the campaign, Jackson kept the slanders from his wife; she did not even realize that the whitewash committee had solicited depositions from old family friends attesting to her virtue and the regularity of the marriage. Rachel learned of her defense by accident, shortly after the completion of the canvass. The shock of seeing her character discussed in public pamphlets may well have hastened her final collapse. Even death did not still the debate. In memory of his beloved wife, Andrew Jackson commissioned a tombstone that assured the world that "a being so gentle and so virtuous slander might wound but could not dishonor."

Images of death constantly flitted before him. As a youth he had escaped them by wild indulgence; age, social prominence, and custom denied him that release now. Everywhere he turned there were reminders of his own mortality. The public expected him to remain in "deep mourning"; they sent tokens of their sympathy and respect. "Your invaluable present will aid me in my preparation to unite with her in the realms above," read one of Jackson's notes to a well-wisher. Public accolades bore the message: "Old Hickory," "Old Hero," "Old Chieftain," old, old, old. He was old, at sixty-one the oldest man ever elected to the presidency and perhaps the most unhealthy. Although standing six-feet-one, he weighed barely 140 pounds. He suffered from stomach distress and fevers, legacies of his forays into the Alabama forests. To alleviate his cramps and pains, he took liberal doses of sugar of lead, adding more heavy metal to a system that already bore two leaden bullets. Periodic headaches, distorted vision, extreme shortness of breath, swelling of the legs—all suggest possible kidney and heart ailments. Frequent pulmonary abscesses caused internal hemorrhaging, violent coughs, and pleuritis, which sent sharp pains jabbing up his side. Jackson bore these afflictions, but always with the thought "that my time cannot be long here on earth." Such fatalism comforted the guilt-ridden husband who could not understand why the shafts aimed at him had killed his wife instead.

The suffering, the pain, the anguish might have incapacitated a man less bent on retribution. Indeed, there were times when Jackson wished "to spend my days in silent sorrow," "at the tomb of my wife," "in peace from the toils and strife of this world." A sense of duty kept him from this communion. "I cannot retire with propriety," he claimed. "My friends draged me before the public contrary to my wishes . . . to perpetuate the blessings of liberty to our country and to put down misrule." Tragedy thus magnified Jackson's fears of conspiracy and renewed his sense of self-righteous mission. But there was an added urgency now. "My enfeebled health and constitution . . . admonished me that it was time that I should place my earthly house in order and prepare for another."

Within weeks of his inauguration in March 1829, Jackson's earthly house stood in utter disarray as the result of a social scandal that the new president took far more seriously than have the guardians of his historical reputation. The "Eaton Affair" (Or "Eaton Malaria," as John Quincy Adams called it) involved the social ostracism of Mrs. John Eaton, wife of Jackson's confidant and new secretary of war. In rallying to Mrs. Eaton's defense, the president was not indulging some private quirk nor methodically preparing a political purge. He considered his own reputation at stake. By defending feminine virtue, he hoped to avenge the slanders of the campaign and put down the forces of corruption. No small task, the effort would shape his entire presidency.

The Eaton affair originated in conflicting views of social order and revealed the depths of Jackson's animosity for

Washington politics. The new president had little respect for conventions and customs in the nation's capital. He did not understand the artificial society that had taken hold in this community of transients. The intrigues, the gossips, the social snubs, the incessant rankings and rerankings of respectability that were important diversions in this isolated outpost held little interest for him. Not that Jackson was antisocial; until Rachel's death the Hermitage literally thronged with visitors, sometimes nearly fifty a day. But the host understood his guests; they honored him by their presence. Jackson found little honor in Washington. "There is nothing done here but vissiting and *carding each other,*" he complained to Rachel during his brief term as senator in 1823. "You know how much I was disgusted with these scenes, when you and I were here." The disgust was fed by the frontiersman's fear that he was unwelcome in polite society and by the suspicion that social prejudices had played an important part in several running battles with his Washington enemies. Jackson saw a direct link between political corruption and social intrigue.

As president, Jackson fully intended to shield himself from these evils by "the council and society of my dear wife." When Rachel died, he surrounded himself with other relatives and Tennessee friends, who soon became the talk of the capital. Rachel's nephew Andrew Jackson Donelson came to Washington as the president's private secretary. Donelson's wife, Emily, a beautiful but somewhat naive woman, took over as social mistress of the new administration with considerably more enthusiasm than Rachel would have displayed. The president's closest Tennessee confidant was William B. Lewis, his former army quartermaster. Lewis's shady dealings in Indian lands had previously prompted considerable criticism, especially during the presidential campaign. Jackson never was a very good judge of character, especially of those who claimed his friendship. He not only brought Lewis to Washington; he gave him permanent lodging in the White House. Along with later arrivals Amos Kendall and Francis P. Blair, this coterie of Westerners enjoyed so much access to the president that critics soon invented a cabal of their own: the kitchen cabinet.

No presidential associate generated more controversy than the former senator from Tennessee, John Eaton. In part the animosity was pure jealousy. As Jackson's campaign manager, Eaton played a prominent role in the selection of the cabinet, a task that always enlivened the preinaugural atmosphere by stimulating appetites and expectations. Although he had sworn to oppose secrecy and intrigue, Jackson chose his cabinet without consulting key party leaders, not even those from his own state. Far from putting an end to political maneuvering, the selections furthered the ambitions of Martin Van Buren and John C. Calhoun. The New Yorker agreed to become secretary of state, the post traditionally held by the heir-apparent. The vice-president contented himself with the support of the second most powerful cabinet official, Pennsylvania's Samuel Ingham, the new secretary of the treasury. In appointing North Carolina's John P. Branch as secretary of the navy and Georgia's John M. Berrien as attorney general, Jackson sparked renewed criticism of a corrupt compact between the legislature and the executive. Actually, neither man had enjoyed much influence during his tenure in Congress.

Having made the customary bows to political fealty and sectional balance, Jackson reserved one cabinet position for a close personal friend. He offered the War Department to his Tennessee associates Hugh Lawson White and John Eaton with the understanding that the two men would decide between them who would be the president's confidant. Eaton desperately wanted the post. White was either too polite or disgusted with the selection procedure to stand in the way. Eaton had his cherished cabinet appointment, Jackson had his personal confidant, and the capital had a social tempest more powerful than the inaugural bacchanal. "It is heart-rending to reflect," wrote one injured participant two years later, "that such may be the consequence of an incident that was at first too trifling to name; but it is now important enough to agitate the country and involve in its consequences the peace of families and the destiny of a great name and still greater public interests."

To the protectors of Washington's moral standards, John Eaton's appointment was no trifling matter. The middle-aged widower's marriage to the twenty-nine-year-old daughter of a local tavern keeper offended their sense of social order. Not that the new nation's social arbiters had a prejucice against tavern keepers; the son of one was about to become secretary of state. But for all his political machinations, Martin Van Buren was discreet. The new Mrs. Eaton was not.

Born at the turn of the century, Peggy O'Neale came to know the great and near great who frequented her father's inn. Her vivacious flirtations and uncommon beauty captivated lonely politicians, drove her first husband, a navy purser, to flee to the Mediterranean, and even sparked some gallant enthusiasm from Old Hickory himself, who at Eaton's urging stayed at the O'Neale establishment in 1823. Eaton was the most taken. He agreed to manage Peggy's business affairs. In the fall of 1828 her husband committed suicide in an obscure overseas port, and John Eaton volunteered to give Peggy his good name, a gift that mounting rumors of adultery would soon depreciate. Before his march to the altar, Eaton asked Jackson's blessing; the president-elect encouraged the alliance, claiming in a fit of romantic optimism that it would silence all the wagging tongues. Far from doing that, the wedding prompted snide remarks of "what a suitable lady in waiting Mrs. Eaton will make to Mrs. Jackson . . . birds of a feather will flock together." News of Rachel's death led many Washington socialites to assume that Mrs. Eaton would wait no longer in her quest for social power and prestige.

The first prominent member of the administration to confront the delicate problem of whether to socialize with the Eatons was Vice-President John C. Calhoun, whose presidential ambitions necessitated the awkward pose that he had long been Jackson's defender, even during the heated cabinet debates on the Seminole War. Calhoun's enemies, particularly William B. Lewis and the growing number of Van Buren adherents around the president, were all too eager to prove Calhoun faithless. Neither the vice-president nor his detractors controlled events. Had not Floride Calhoun turned on her heel, had not the cabinet wives joined in this *"noble* stand" by refusing to "visit one, who has left her strait and narrow path," the crisis might have been averted.

The stand was on grounds of high moral principle and soon drew support from the minister of the largest Washington congregation. The protest was not politically staged. No Machiavellian manipulator maneuvered astute, strong-willed women like Floride Calhoun, who fully realized the political chaos that would result from their decisions but considered social respectability more important than politics. Their husbands desperately wanted a return to domestic bliss. Protest against the president's social standards gave rise to the storm; Andrew Jackson's fury blew the protest to gale force. Only when at its height did it spawn the whirlwinds of ambition and collusion.

Had the president been able to summon a measure of detachment he might have realized what some of his good friends came to see—that involvement in the Eaton embroglio was beneath the dignity of his office. In the aftermath of Rachel's death, such objectivity was impossible. Andrew Jackson regarded the presidency, not as an institution with certain inherent customs and responsibilities, but as vindication of his injured reputation, a reward for his faithful service. As long as the slanders continued, he remained the candidate, courting public favor, seeking moral revenge. But this time he would direct his own defense.

Jackson personalized the issue immediately. This was more than a contest over social etiquette; it was a clear case of intimidation, the work of "Clay and his minions" who had tried unsuccessfully to prevent his election and were now attempting to prevent Eaton from taking his rightful place in the cabinet. Jackson refused to cast Eaton aside, just as he refused to believe any of the stories circulated by these corrupt political gossip-mongers. Eaton was an honorable man; his wife was therefore above suspicion. "It was enough for his friends to know that he had married her to put down the slang of the gossips of the city." The wedding did not silence the defamers any more than Jackson's own marriage had spared Rachel nearly three decades of anguish. He would have to demonstrate Peggy's innocence just as conclusively as the whitewash committee had proved Rachel's purity. By doing so Jackson would complete the defense of feminine virtue begun during the campaign, remove any lingering doubts about his own commitment to social order, and absolve some of the awful guilt brought on by Rachel's death.

These deeply personal motives indicate that for Andrew Jackson, at least, the Eaton affair was no mere maneuver designed to oust Calhoun and other dissidents from the administration. Had he been bent on such a straightforward political mission, the president would no doubt have behaved differently during his first year in office. For one thing, he tried to silence all the gossip rather than exploit it for partisan advantage. For nearly six months Jackson played the moral inquisitor, privately investigating the charges against Peggy Eaton. Whether writing to obtain affidavits on the causes of her husband's suicide, sending agents to a New York hotel to check on rumors of Eaton's impropriety, or personally interrogating the Washington pastor who lent credence to the slanders, Jackson played the part denied him during the campaign. He wrote long letters in Peggy's defense, recorded a narrative of his investigations, and in the fall of 1829 held one of the most bizarre cabinet meetings in American history.

Having accumulated evidence to prove Peggy's innocence, the president summoned her accusers before the cabinet and tried to force them to recant, hoping that his councilors would then end their social boycott of the first family. The arraignment proceeded very badly. Two frightened ministers sat under Jackson's irate gaze, explaining that they had originally brought the rumors to the president's attention to save him embarrassment. Jackson wanted none of their good intentions; he demanded a recantation. During the course of these exceptional deliberations, the Reverend Ezra Styles Ely said that his own inquiries proved John Eaton innocent of any wrongdoing. "And Mrs. Eaton also!" the president broke in. "On that point I would rather not give an opinion," Ely replied. "She is chaste as a virgin," Jackson roared and soon disbanded the meeting in disgust.

After this abortive tribunal, the storm entered its most devastating phase. When Congress reassembled in December 1829, rumors circulated that Peggy Eaton was unwelcome at all social functions, including those given by the diplomatic corps. Additional stories told of deep rifts in the cabinet and hinted that Jackson had lost control of his administration. In a sense all the gossip was true. When concerned congressmen questioned the president about the dissension, Jackson struck out blindly in all directions; he thought of banishing recalcitrant foreign diplomats and dismissing the cabinet in toto, thereby proving his mastery. Talked out of these desperate measures, he nevertheless began to judge officials by their social behavior. Those who accorded Mrs. Eaton the respect due her station fared well in his estimation. Those who supported the continuing social ostracism Jackson consigned to the vast conspiracy that grew daily. No one escaped scrutiny, not even his relatives. Jackson insisted that Emily Donelson call on Mrs. Eaton. "My duty is that my household should bestow equal comity to all," Jackson lectured, "and the nation expects me to controle my household to this rule." Emily refused to be badgered. In the fall of 1830, she and her husband reluctantly left the president's house. Jackson grieved at their departure, attributing it to "a want of experience and the corruption of the world." "I am thrown upon strangers," he moaned, "instead of those I took great pains in education that they might be a comfort & aid to me, in my declining years."

The president endured these defections as he endured physical torment, with a conviction of self-righteousness that at times bordered on obsession. Jackson was always prone to elevate private problems to the level of public issues, but as a result of Rachel's death and the attacks on Mrs. Eaton, he had even greater difficulty discriminating between personal duty and national honor, between family and country. "Was this proper treatment to me as President of the United States, and by those representing me as such in the place of my departed wife," he demanded to know after the Donelson's departure. "Was this proper as head of the family, & they in the place of my children?"

These doubts far more than any concern for ideology or party policy determined Andrew Jackson's behavior during his first term of office. Whether as spoilsman, government reformer, defender of strict construction, architect of Indian removal, or enemy of the Bank, the president acted more in self-defense than out of loyalty to the Democratic coalition.

In some respects, Andrew Jackson's quest for vindication served the party well. Without a positive platform, the Democratic alliance relied upon state political organizations like the Albany Regency and the Richmond Junto. These crude machines in turn derived their authority from controlling state legislatures and carefully dispensing patronage. Within each state, federal offices constituted a significant source of reward for the party faithful. Postmasters, district attorneys, collectors of customs, land agents—these were but a few of the important federal posts coveted by state partisans. Systematic catering might not satiate these appetites, but it could prevent the party from devouring itself.

Consumed by fears of intrigue, corrupt bargains, and conspiracy, Andrew Jackson entered office determined to achieve political reform by use of his patronage powers. He spoke often of appointments and removals but never as a source of party solidarity, never as the "spoils" of victory. Such realism ran counter to his belief that politics was dirty business. He thought of himself not as a methodical spoilsman but as the righteous avenger, whose task it was to "cleanse the Augean Stables." The classical imagery neatly conveys the sense of duty and distaste that he brought to the job. Furthermore, Jackson believed that his enemies had left the stables "in such a state" just "to embarrass me." He would not tolerate the contamination for long. "You know when I am excited all my energies come forth," he assured his friend John Coffee.

The transfer of power did bring forth his energies. In his first few months in office, Jackson gave every indication that he intended to sweep out all the "rats" that he believed had infested federal offices during the Adams administration. After observing these reforms Jackson's predecessor bitterly remarked, "To feed the cormorant appetite for place, and to reward the prostitution of canvassing defamers, are the only principles yet discernible in the conduct of the President." The sheer magnitude of this appetite soon drove Jackson to despair: "If I had a tit for every applicant to suck the Treasury pap, all would go away satisfied, but as there are not office for more than one out of five hundred who apply, many must go away dissatisfied." Despite his disenchantment with such maternal dispensation Jackson vowed to carry on. "All I can do is, select honest and competant men." At times Jackson selected men who were neither honest nor competent. Samuel Gwin, a land agent in the Southwest, openly speculated in government revenues; Samuel Swartwout, collector of customs in the Port of New York, absconded with $1,250,000. Ironically, at the time of his appointment Swartwout had urged the president to propose legislation that would relieve bankrupt merchants.

In view of these disastrous appointments, the Democratic coalition may have been fortunate that circumstances prevented the president from making a clean sweep. In his two terms in office, Jackson removed no more than a fifth of all federal office holders, including over a third of those requiring Senate confirmation. Although slightly higher than comparable figures for the Jefferson administrations, these statistics clearly indicate that Jackson did not originate the spoils system or carry it to extremes. During the first two years of the new coalition's rule, a time when the transfer of power stimulated the most heated patronage battles, the president was plagued by miserable health and concentrated his limited energies on the Eaton affair. Doubtless a vigorous, less preoccupied Jackson would have pushed reforms even further, for he was constantly referring to the need to purge the government of its accumulated wickedness. Doubtless, too, Jackson considered the defense of feminine virtue equally as important as the removal of federal officeholders. They were related tasks. By upholding the bonds of friendship, by raising the social standards of the Washington community, by putting down the vicious slanders against Peggy Eaton, Jackson believed that he was serving the cause of reform just as surely as when he replaced a corrupt man with an honest one.

In December 1829, Jackson invited Congress to join the crusade by adopting the principle of rotation in office. Again his fears of corruption predominated. "There are, perhaps, few who can for any length of time enjoy office and power without being more or less under the influence of feelings unfavorable to the faithful discharge of their public duties." Jackson proposed that the "length of time" be set at four years. Such a limitation would eliminate the experienced servant, but then the president believed that "the duties of all public officials are so plain that men of intelligence may readily qualify themselves . . . and . . . more is lost by the long continuation of men in office than is generally to be gained by their experience." Jackson showed little sympathy for the individual distress that might accompany rotation; "he who is removed has the same means of obtaining a living that are enjoyed by the millions who never held office."

The political realist would interpret the president's suggestions as a thinly disguised attempt to increase executive patronage. Indeed, many of Jackson's contemporary critics raised this objection, enough so that Congress refused to endorse rotation. Clearly, the president's distrust of political jobbery outweighed any thought of partisan advantage, as it did in his concurrent proposal that Congress alter the mode of presidential election. When Jackson recommended that the House of Representatives have no role in the electoral process, that the president be chosen by popular majority, that his term be fixed by law at six years, and that, failing these modifications, all congressmen be prohibited from "appointments in the gift of the President" they helped select, Jackson was merely registering his disgust with the "corrupt bargain" of 1825.

The president's preoccupation with corruption and his belief that he was the target of congressional abuse had an equally telling impact on his handling of internal improvements. Late in May 1830, Congress passed and sent to the White House a bill authorizing government purchase of stock in a road to be constructed between Maysville and Lexington, Kentucky. State-rights enthusiasts worried that Jackson might approve this measure and commit the federal government to support additional projects of purely local scope, especially since he had taken no clear stand on the question of internal improvements. Well aware of these apprehensions, Martin Van Buren advised the president to veto the Maysville road bill. Van Buren hoped that disapproval would renew the administration's pledge to curb the power of the central government. Jackson accepted the advice. He had come to appreciate his secretary's political loyalty as well as his polite attentions to Mrs. Eaton.

Thanks to Van Buren's careful wording, the Maysville veto did appear to be based on a strict construction of the Constitution. The message promised to keep the national government "within its proper sphere," allowing "the states to manage their own concerns in their own way." In his own personal draft, Jackson appeared much less concerned with constitutional distinctions and historical precedents, much more worried about endangered liberties and "combinations in Congress." Grant the government the right to buy stock in a state corporation, he argued, and it would soon become an engine of destruction, tampering with "state elections" and "destroying the morals of your people." Encourage such appropriations and congressional standards would further decay, clearing the way for more "flagitious Legislation arising from combinations if you will vote with me I will vote with you so disgraceful to our country." In Jackson's eyes, no one epitomized the pernicious legislative back-scratching more than Kentucky's Henry Clay, architect of the original "corrupt bargain" and the man who stood to gain most from construction of the Maysville Turnpike.

Having taken a symbolic stand against congressional logrolling and having gained revenge at the expense of his archrival from Kentucky, Jackson proceeded to approve more internal improvement bills during his two terms in office than all his predecessors combined. Not that Jackson suddenly overcame his fears of corruption or that he developed a more charitable view of human nature; most of the bills he approved were recommended by army engineers and were therefore acceptable. In addition, the president found in Indian affairs another outlet for his anxieties.

Few American presidents have taken such personal initiative in domestic affairs as Andrew Jackson took in Indian removal. "That great work was emphatically the fruit of his own exertions," Van Buren recalled sometime later. "It was his judgment, his experience, his indomitable vigor and unrelenting activity that secured success." Whereas other chief executives have been inclined to act as their own secretaries of state, Jackson intended to be his own secretary of war. He insisted that a personal friend, a Westerner, head the War Department. When Washington critics began their attacks on John Eaton, the president responded swiftly, in part because he took the criticism personally, but also because he wanted Eaton to press for Indian removal as quickly as possible. Eaton later resigned from the cabinet and Jackson was extremely reluctant to appoint a successor who was "unacquainted with Indian matters." He eventually settled on Michigan's governor Lewis Cass, an outspoken advocate of removal. Likewise, Jackson appointed Georgia's John Berrien as his first attorney general, knowing full well that the collision between that state and the Cherokee Indians would soon require the federal government to take a stand on the thorny question of Indian sovereignty. In addition to these critical appointments, Jackson maintained extensive personal correspondence on Indian affairs. He issued instructions to treaty negotiators, employed trusted advisers like John Coffee to treat with tribesmen, exchanged opinions with Indian agents, and even summoned Indian leaders to his summer residence for private negotiations.

It is tempting to dismiss Andrew Jackson's Indian policy as bigotry pure and simple. To do so is to miss its significance. In these matters, the president embodied contradictions that marred federal policy since the eighteenth century. Always a zealous warrior, Jackson was also something of a missionary at heart. Throughout his career as a military commander and treaty negotiator he had reiterated the hope first expressed on the smouldering Creek battlefields: that out of the ashes would arise a new, peaceful Indian society. This vision had intensely personal origins, but then so did the dreams of many an Indian missionary, for whom conversion of the heathen represented vicarious salvation. Jackson was less captivated by religious visions, more concerned with the secular transformation of warrior to peaceful agrarian. Neither the missionaries nor the president they so actively opposed demonstrated much appreciation for the integrity of Indian culture. In one respect, of course, they differed markedly. The last of the Jeffersonian philanthropists wanted to preserve the Indian tribal lands. By 1829, Jackson, along with a substantial number of American citizens and political leaders, had become thoroughly disenchanted with this traditional approach to the Indian problem. He readily accepted the suggestions of Lewis Cass and others that only a massive migration west of the Mississippi could remove the Indians from the degrading circumstances that had befallen them in the 1820s.

Once committed, Jackson pursued removal relentlessly. In December 1829, at a time when he was critically ill and under intense pressure from Peggy Eaton's detractors, the president formally proposed that Congress guarantee land west of the Mississippi to the Indians and appropriate funds to facilitate removal. "This emigration should be voluntary," Jackson assured Congress, "for it would be as cruel as unjust to compel the aborigines to abandon the graves of their fathers and seek a home in a distant land." With a dispatch rarely duplicated in subsequent deliberations, Congress approved an Indian removal bill in May 1830. The vote was extremely close, indicating the administration's tenuous position in the legislature. Nevertheless, this act was the only major legislative accomplishment of Jackson's first term. As such it demonstrated that support for Indian removal transcended party lines.

By appropriating the sum of $500,000, Congress empowered the president to begin direct negotiations with the southern Indians, offering them a home in the West in exchange for their tribal lands in the East. Jackson wasted little time in acting on this narrow mandate. In August 1830, he personally attended the council session at Franklin, Tennessee, where Eaton and Coffee negotiated a removal treaty with the Chickasaws. A month later these two trusted presidential aides met with the Choctaw Indians at Dancing Rabbit Creek and concluded a treaty that foreshadowed subsequent settlements with the Creeks and Cherokees. Despite the president's emphasis on voluntarism, the treaty commissioners resorted to bribery and intimidation to secure the Choctaw's consent. After the main body of the Choctaw delegation had abandoned the deliberations in disgust, Eaton dickered with a few remaining spokesmen, holding out "special reservations" of land in return for their support. Even the general allotments to heads of families were a form of bribery.

The Jackson administration was willing to confer generous grants on those tribesmen who decided to remain because it cynically calculated that few Choctaws would be able to retain their holdings in the face of white encirclement. Even to claim an allotment, an Indian had to rely upon strange legal codes; if successful in obtaining land, the claimant still had to live there five years before receiving title. Jackson reasoned that the speculators would persuade the Indians to sell long before the waiting period was over. Why else would he tell a prospective Indian agent: "The Government is endeavoring to concentrate the Indians west of the Mississippi and you just turn all your energy to this object—in the course of which, some more profitable business may present itself"? In urging the immediate acquisition and sale of Indian land, Jackson fancied that he was serving the cause of government economy. He hoped to pay for the entire cost of removal from the proceeds of these land sales and avoid increasing a national debt that he had pledged to extinguish. Characteristically, he saw no reason why his friends should not profit from these proceedings. "This will give you employment," Jackson told Coffee after sending one treaty to the Senate.

Previous presidents had sanctioned bribery at the treaty grounds; yet at Dancing Rabbit Creek, Jackson's representatives threatened the Choctaws with a frightening new form of pressure. In a fit of frustration Eaton confirmed what the president had already told Indian agents: either the tribes agreed to move, or they would be left totally at the mercy of state laws, without any legal form of self-government, without any federal protection whatever. From experience, Jackson knew that the nation's meager military establishment could hardly shield the Indians from white avarice and encroachment. As leader of a new coalition pledged to uphold state rights, the president also knew the political hazards of attempting to interfere with the decisions of a determined state regime. Jackson knew full well that the extension of state laws would destroy tribal government. "I was satisfied that the Indians could not possibly live under the laws of the states," he freely admitted in 1830. "If they now refuse to accept the liberal terms offered they can only be liable for whatever evils and difficulties may arise. I feel conscious of having done my duty to my red children," he concluded. In short, Jackson believed that his policy was benevolent. Since the states would force the Indians to move, since he felt powerless to resist such pressure, at least he could see that the Indian received token payment for his land.

Having offered what he considered to be liberal terms, Jackson could not understand Indian resistance. When the Creeks refused to meet their conqueror in 1830 and hired former Attorney General William Wirt to represent them, Jackson exploded: "The course of *Wirt* has been truly wicked. It has been wielded as an engine to prevent the Indians from moving across the Mississippi and will lead to the destruction of the poor ignorant Indians." The president resented Wirt's meddling but consoled himself that wickedness would soon find its own rewards. Meanwhile he was content to leave "the poor deluded Creeks and Cherokees to their fate, and their annihilation, which their wicked advisors has induced." Even when successful in overcoming Indian resistance, Jackson saw the "serpent" at work. In August 1830, after receiving news of the Treaty of Franklin, Jackson reported, "Thus far we have succeeded against the most corrupt and secret combination that ever did exist, and we have preserved my Chickasaw friends and red brethren."

In Jackson's view, the West offered the Indians a permanent home and Americans permanent relief from racial tensions. Like many of his contemporaries, the president regarded the vast trans-Mississippi region as a geographical nirvana. There a new Indian civilization would arise, secure in its right to the land, freed from the evils of alcohol, educated in the virtues of agrarian pursuits, and, above all, isolated from white society. Significantly, Jackson looked to the Army to keep peace and help maintain the new social order. This vision was no mere afterthought of the removal policy, but a clear expression of Jackson's disgust with the social decay he perceived affecting Indians and whites alike. "How many thousands of our own people would gladly embrace the opportunity of removing to the west on such conditions!" he asked in outlining federal support for removal.

Andrew Jackson took particular pride in "that great work," to use Van Buren's terms, because by removing the Indians, he believed he was exonerating "the national character from all imputation." In the success of his Indian removal policies, Jackson saw a measure of personal vindication as well. Unable to prove Peggy Eaton "chaste as a Virgin," nor able to "cleanse the Augean Stables," silence slander, preserve family harmony, or achieve other reforms he considered essential to his and the nation's well-being, he could at least take satisfaction from this act. He continued to perceive himself as a "slave to office." Surrounded by corruption, tormented by sickness, and deserted by family, he found rare release in asserting his authority over his "red children." But the president's satisfaction was short-lived. By the time his "friends and brothers" embarked on their "Trail of Tears," their "great father the President" found himself in a new war against corruption, this time on a strange, almost alien battlefield.

VI

The Bank:
"I Will Kill It"

THE MOTIVE SEEMS disarmingly simple. "The Bank, Mr. Van Buren, is trying to kill me, but I will kill it." This emphatic declaration was lost in the heat of battle; recent debate has relegated it to the status of interesting but insignificant theatrics. Explanations of the Bank War abound, tracing its origins to the expansion of the American economy, the rivalry of state machines, the selfish actions of entrepreneurs "on the make," and the conflict between social classes. One economist even contends that all the sound and fury signified nothing, that Bank War or no Bank War the cycle of inflation and depression would have descended on the United States in the 1830s. His figures do not lie, but they do not tell us very much either, not about the real causes of a struggle that would have a profound impact on the American political system for years to come. Without Andrew Jackson, without his fears, his anger, his boldness, his ambivalence, there might never have been a war at all. The president carried out his threat; he killed the Bank. But it was hardly a case of premeditated murder. As he so graphically told his former secretary of state, he considered it a matter of self-defense.

Jackson did not enter office a convert to hard money. Certainly his several flirtations with bankruptcy had produced a lifelong fear of insolvency and distrust of paper money. Jackson distrusted the Indians, too, but he welcomed them as allies in 1814, a year in which he also used state banks to extend credit and facilitate provisioning of his troops. In 1818, he praised the "Patriotism" of the "Branch Bank" in Nashville and urged President Monroe to keep government revenues on deposit there. Jackson freely admitted at this time that he held stock in the "Nashville Bank, the only Bank stock I own." Even after the Panic of 1819 produced a nationwide outcry against "overbanking" and forced Jackson himself to question the constitutionality of a national bank, he used his offices as governor of Florida to transmit a petition that the Second Bank of the United States establish a branch in Pensacola.

As a planter, speculator, and erstwhile merchant, Jackson continued to deal in bank notes long after his financial fiasco in Philadelphia in 1795, when his use of credit nearly left him penniless. At one time in 1819, his accounts showed several sizable transactions using notes as large as $5,000. He bought land, purchased slaves, and built a handsome plantation house with the assistance of bank paper. Though his fortunes began to dwindle in the 1820s, he continued to keep his funds in banks and transacted his personal affairs by drafts and notes. All the while he complained about the "paper system that will ruin the state."

Jackson did not hate all paper money, only the excessive note issues that threatened to depreciate his holdings. "I therefore protest against receiving any of that trash," he said of the Tennessee bank bill in 1821, admitting that he would "take the old state bank or its branches, at the exchange for Orleans." The general mustered similar anger against the relief laws aimed at helping insolvent debtors grapple with the hardships following the Panic of 1819. Privately, Jackson contemplated taking advantage of those laws to combat his own financial setbacks. This growing ambivalence is found in advice to his nephew Andrew Jackson Donelson. "Dollars and cents are the legal money of the United States," the Old Hero lectured, "paper money is not." Jackson closed the letter with assurances that if Donelson needed money, "I will raise it by a note on Bank."

Nor did Old Hickory shun the company of bankers and speculators. His confidant John Coffee became one of the most successful entrepreneurs in the Gulf states, creating the Cypress Land Company in 1818 and founding the town of Florence, Alabama. Jackson originally owned stock in Coffee's enterprise; precisely how much remains a mystery, because fire destroyed the records in 1827. Jackson's other Tennessee friends had equally strong ties with the state's financial institutions. John Overton helped found the first state bank in Tennessee and served as a director of the Nashville branch of the Bank of the United States. John Eaton and William B. Lewis also sat on the board of directors. Hugh Lawson White, Jackson's east Tennessee ally who twice refused a cabinet post, presided over a powerful bank in Knoxville. These men retained their ties to the state's financial institutions well into the 1830s.

Amid the confusion of thought and the incongruity of behavior, one emotion was stable. "I cannot sleep indebted," Jackson once confided to Coffee. As he turned more of his attention to politics, Jackson's financial resources declined. His own crops at the Hermitage returned an uncertain profit. "For the last two years I have had no control over my expences and it has exceded my means," he complained shortly before the election of 1828. He had further difficulty managing his ward's estate in Alabama and finally was forced to sell it.

Voters shared Jackson's financial fears just as they shared his distrust of politics. They never expected him to draw up a coherent fiscal program. The nation boasted no council of economic advisors, nor did it recognize economics as a distinct intellectual discipline. The American people viewed financial affairs through the prism of custom and local culture. What they could not explain as the result of religion or the forces of nature, they often blamed on immoral influences or irrational interventions. To those troubled by financial uncertainties, "monsters" stalked the American landscape, menacing economic stability, destroying family solidarity, trampling religious values, stampeding citizens, and breeding a species of corrupt, monopolistic offspring that, if not destroyed, would perpetually threaten traditional liberties. Only in the language of the grotesque could a troubled nation express its innermost anxieties.

Jackson often spoke that language. In vowing to combat corruption, he appealed to those fears. Advisors and state politicians might have thought of personal profit and financial gain, but Jackson rarely mentioned such matters. In his mind and in the minds of many of his supporters, economic dislocation was a product of misdirected ambition and uncontrolled expansion. Once at war with such an unprincipled enemy there could be no temporizing or thought of personal aggrandizement. To Jackson the monsters always had a particularly ferocious bent. Although he did not enter office pledged to slay the hated beasts, he soon came to believe that they were intent on devouring him.

The Second Bank of the United States had not always been that "Monster on Chestnut Street." Like its Federalist forerunner, the Bank performed essential services for the government and the public at large. It stored government revenues, arranged for the transfer of federal funds from one part of the country to another, helped obtain favorable terms for payment of the national debt, and by its redemption policies, acted as a brake on the note issue of state banks. Congress granted the Second Bank a twenty-year charter in 1816 to check the rampant inflation that had swept the country since the expiration of the First Bank five years earlier. With its eighteen branches located in fourteen states and in the District of Columbia, the Second Bank was able to exert considerable influence on the nation's exchanges. To combat the excessive paper money issues of the war years, the Bank tried to force state banks to resume specie payments. As a result of mismanagement and administrative incompetence, the Second Bank only accelerated the deflation that eventually resulted in the Panic of 1819.

The magnitude of this collapse, the widespread social disruption it caused, and its appearance on the heels of postwar prosperity caught Americans unaware. Casting about for causes, they selected the Bank of the United States, whose uncertain leadership and seemingly endless power made it a perfect scapegoat. With a capital stock of $35 million, the Bank was the nation's most powerful financial institution. Private investors controlled four-fifths of this amount; the Treasury held the remainder. The power structure of the Bank mirrored this financial division: twenty directors were selected by the private stockholders; five were appointed by the federal government. The president of the Bank, who appointed the principal officers in each of the branches, exerted considerably more power over the nation's banking system than could the president of the United States. The Bank's power was often more apparent than real. Its president, like the nation's president, had to cope with the severe limitations of a primitive communications network. Although the parent bank in Philadelphia might issue instructions to various branch officers, orders traveled slowly; some never reached their destination. Branch directors might pledge allegiances to the Philadelphia directorate, but they always had to remain responsive to the needs of the locality they served. Furthermore, the Bank and its branches did not stand alone in the fiscal forest. State banks and private corporations vied for public business and were eager to capitalize on the Bank's financial or administrative errors. When the Philadelphia leadership did manage to impose a uniform policy throughout the system, rival banks often complained, especially if that policy restricted their note issue. The Bank was thus vulnerable to charges of "overbanking" as well as "underbanking."

Despite these criticisms, the Second Bank had rebounded after the Panic of 1819. Its supporters felt that the best way to

stifle further opposition would be to press for an early recharter. With a renewed lease on public confidence, the Second Bank would be able to operate more efficiently to curb
inflation and promote stability. A substantial number of
Democrats recognized the Bank's importance. A founder of
the New York State safety fund system, Martin Van Buren had
no quarrel with Chestnut Street. In some respects, the goals
of the safety fund resembled those of the Bank: to guard
against proliferation of unstable banks and to provide adequate reserves in time of financial stringency. Not that Van
Buren defended the Bank or even advocated renewal of the
charter; he simply saw no reason to agitate an issue that need
not arise until 1836. John C. Calhoun was of a similar mind,
as were Jackson's close associates John Overton, John Eaton,
and William B. Lewis.

As on so many other issues, the candidate remained non-
committal during the campaign of 1828. The Second Bank
tried to enlist his friendship by sending a representative to
Tennessee in 1827 to solicit his advice on the proper management of the branch recently opened in Nashville. Jackson refused to be drawn into a discussion, claiming that he had never
"been, in any manner, connected with Banks." In fact, Jackson
had been "connected" with banks and did harbor suspicions
about the operations of the Nashville branch. Even though
Overton served on the board of directors, Jackson believed
rumors that his political enemies had been given access to his
bankbook. Had this been the opposition's only political crime,
the candidate might well have focused his anger on the Bank
question. As it was, he was preoccupied with a multitude of
campaign slanders.

In the aftermath of the election, Jackson talked fleetingly of
making some declaration against the Bank. Two successive
crop failures contributed to his growing depression. "I am
now and have been for some time without money," he wrote
in the fall of 1828. "The low price of cotton left me indebted
and the ravages of the worm upon my present crop, I fear, will

render me unable to close my necessary accounts at the end of this year." Before he could begin this reckoning, Rachel died, plunging him deeper into despair. Distracted by personal tragedy, bewildered by the unanticipated volume of patronage problems, and deeply troubled by the Eaton affair, Jackson made no mention of the Second Bank in his inaugural address. In forming the cabinet, the new president displayed none of the anti-Bank animus evident in his later behavior. The secretary of the treasury, the cabinet official most responsible for fiscal policy, came from Pennsylvania and was an avowed supporter of the Bank. Attorney General John Berrien had been a legal representative for the branch bank in Savannah, Georgia. The president's other councillors had no reason to contest a recharter.

As the Eaton affair wore on and Jackson became convinced that his enemies would stop at nothing to destroy his reputation, he began to place more credence in recurring rumors that the Bank, through its branches, had illegally intervened in the election of 1828 and thus indirectly assailed his reputation. The first of these alleged interventions concerned the branch banks in Lexington and Louisville, Kentucky. The president was easily persuaded that Henry Clay—"The Judas of the West"—had not only received his thirty pieces of silver but was storing them in a branch bank and using this corrupt currency to buy votes.

Jackson did not rush to the attack. Throughout the spring and summer of 1829, his health was precarious, his breathing so labored that it pained visitors to be in the same room with him. According to his secretary, this combination of failing health and immense social tension did "more to paralyze his energies than years of regular and simple operations of the Gov. ought to have done." Jackson rallied for a time in the fall of 1829, spending untold hours interrogating Peggy Eaton's detractors, preparing at the same time to press for congressional approval of Indian removal. With his remaining strength, Jackson began a series of inquiries about possible substitutes for the Second Bank. While in the process of this investigation, he had his first formal meeting with the Bank's president, Nicholas Biddle.

At first glance, the antagonists seem remarkably different. Nearly twenty years Jackson's junior, Nicholas Biddle looked the part of the prosperous banker. His round, romantic face framed by curly brown hair, his delicate complexion belying an avid interest in farming, his dress and bearing always proper, almost aristocratic, Biddle gave the impression of being a highly cultivated dilettante. He was exceptionally well educated. Although trained as a lawyer, Biddle believed himself a scholar, and he spent long hours translating Greek and French poetry. He also contributed to magazines, served as editor of *Port Folio,* and wrote his own verse. In 1823, when critics charged that the thirty-six-year-old Philadelphian was too young to become president of the Second Bank and that his talents were literary, not financial, Biddle the poet replied:

> I prefer my last letter from Barings or Hope
> To the finest epistles of Pliny or Pope.

Pretentious and arrogant though he was, Biddle was neither impractical nor incurably romantic.

While the president kept his ambivalent financial views to himself, Biddle wasted no opportunity to announce his nationalistic opinions. He advocated direct government sponsorship of internal improvements, favored a protective tariff, and argued that the development of American manufacturers would free the country from the economic tyranny of England. Above all, he wanted to use the Bank to combat such ruinous fluctuations in the economy as the Panic of 1819. Biddle believed that he had rescued the nation from the depths of this disaster by changing the loan structure of the Bank and making more money available for circulation. At the same time, he prided himself on being a conservative financier, whose refusal to encourage real estate speculation operated in the country's best interest.

The president and the banker actually had a good deal more in common than their backgrounds or experience indicated. Although Biddle aspired to be a power broker, he shared Jackson's distrust of politics, on several occasions remarking that he intended to keep the Bank above partisan conflict. Both men were prone to see conspiracies; these anxieties justified a descent from the lofty heights of statesmanship to the vulgar pit of politics. The decline began shortly after their meeting in the fall of 1829.

Jackson was the first to descend. During their lengthy interview, he virtually promised to mention the Bank favorably in the forthcoming annual message. This tribute was to be in appreciation for the Bank's services in helping to liquidate the national debt. Biddle had even catered to Jackson's vanity by scheduling the final payment on the eighteenth anniversary of the Battle of New Orleans. Biddle may have appraised Jackson's conceit accurately, but he totally underestimated the president's obsession with corruption and conspiracy. The Philadelphia financier had personally investigated the campaign charges against his branch directors in Louisville and Lexington, Kentucky, and found no evidence of electoral tampering. He hoped the president would take this testimony at face value. Jackson accepted nothing at face value, especially not the "verity of the directors" who had refused to be held accountable to the administration.

Had Jackson and Biddle met more often, they might have been able to resolve such misunderstandings and reach some mutually acceptable agreement on the Bank's future. As it was, they worked through intermediaries, many of whom distorted information to suit their own inflated vanities. Amos Kendall, a former Kentucky newspaper editor and persistent anti-Bank critic, continued to feed Jackson's suspicions of the Bank's interference in western elections. New Hampshire's Isaac Hill, an equally partisan, equally persistent journalist, relayed similar stories about the Branch Bank in Portsmouth. Ironically, Biddle had less to fear from these avowed enemies than from counselors like William B. Lewis, who professed friendship to the Bank, claimed to represent the president's views, and regularly issued optimistic statements that Jackson would agree to a recharter if Biddle would make a few minor changes in the Bank's structure.

The president's first annual message came as a shock to Nicholas Biddle, but it was hardly the opening salvo of the Bank War. Instead of expressing gratitude for debt service, Jackson questioned whether the Bank was constitutional and claimed that "it has failed in the great end of establishing a uniform and sound currency." He further recommended that Congress consider a new bank "founded upon the credit of the government and its revenues." Biddle was miffed, not so much at the charges; he had heard them all before. Nor did he fear a new banking plan that was "too bad to find any partisans." Rather he resented the loss of control. He had come away from the Washington meeting convinced that he had captured the president's good will and no doubt fancying that he had captivated the Old Hero by his flatteries. Instead of admitting his miscalculations, Biddle rationalized that Jackson spoke only for himself, not for his party.

In a sense Biddle was correct; Jackson's message was more personal bias than partisan policy. Despite the contemplation of a variety of alternative banking schemes, despite his consultation with several prominent Democrats, the president had no clear plan for a new bank, nor did he recommend any to Congress. The report of the secretary of the treasury, the usual vehicle for such proposals, mentioned neither the Second Bank nor Jackson's criticism. When the House Ways and Means Committee came to the pertinent paragraphs near the end of the president's message, they refused to take Jackson seriously, rejecting any idea of a government bank but praising the president's "disinterested patriotism" and "exalted character."

Distracted patriotism might have been a more appropriate description of Jackson's mood and motive. He felt bound to take notice of the corruption around him, to indicate its link with the financial aristocracy. At the same time, he hesitated to touch off a lengthy, acrimonious debate in Congress. With the Bank's charter not due to expire until 1836, Jackson had little hope of creating a new government bank during his presidency, especially since he had promised to serve only one term. Moreover, Jackson usually fought his battles one at a time; in December 1829, he was intent on securing passage of the Indian removal bill and for that reason limited his remarks on the Bank to vague generalities. Like his call for popular election of the president, Jackson's statement on the Bank seems more an extension of his aversion to corrupt politics than a considered policy proposal.

Even if the president had the will, he lacked the strength. In December 1829, he fell desperately ill, his feet and hands so swollen that he "appeared to be rapidly assuming the character of a *confirmed dropsy.*" He waged a quiet, desperate struggle to regain his health; the effort drained his energy and diverted his attention. When he did recover early in 1830, the president concentrated on Indian removal and internal improvements. Jackson returned to the subject of the Bank in his second annual message, reiterating his earlier statements and slightly amplifying his suggestions for a government bank. As if fearful that even this moderate expansion might be regarded as a definite plan, Jackson closed:

These suggestions are not made so much as a recommendation as with a view of calling the attention of Congress to the possible modifications of a system which cannot continue to exist in its present form without . . . perpetual apprehensions and discontent on the part of the States and the people.

Here was an open invitation to compromise.

Although their associates were willing to resolve the dispute, neither Biddle nor Jackson had left enough leeway to change course. Both men had authorized propaganda campaigns involving lengthy discussions in the press. When Jackson became dissatisfied with Duff Green's support for Calhoun and the Bank, he arranged for Kentucky's Francis P. Blair to come to the capital as editor of the *Washington Globe*. This new paper soon replaced the *United States Telegraph* as the administration's journalistic organ, just as Blair replaced Green in the president's inner circle. For his part, Biddle saw nothing wrong with paying to have pro-Bank stories circulated in opposition papers. "If a grocer wishes to apprize the public that he has a fresh supply of figs," Biddle argued, "the printer whom he employs for that purpose never thinks of giving his labor for nothing." Biddle did not give a fig about reassurances from the White House. His Bank had been attacked in the president's annual message and he wanted to set the record straight. To Jackson, these spirited defenses represented positive proof that the Bank was playing politics in violation of its charter. This journalistic jousting had little effect on the formulation of policy or on public opinion, but it indicated that Biddle and Jackson had each assumed a defensive position, making subsequent negotiations extremely difficult.

At no time did these negotiations look more promising than in 1831. Ironically, the cause for optimism was a total reorganization of the cabinet. For over two years, the president had endured the social hostilities generated by the Eaton affair. He never once acknowledged the legitimacy of any of the charges against Mrs. Eaton; nevertheless, he grew weary of the incessant turmoil, especially since it deprived him of the company of his family. Jackson also tired of the criticism that he was bent on becoming a tyrant by ruling without the advice of his council. The president stopped holding cabinet meetings for only one reason: to reduce the possibility of creating further animosity in an administration already rent by discord. He knew full well that he was running away from the problem of internal dissension, that such evasion made him vulnerable to charges of executive usurpation. The president sincerely wanted to restore administrative harmony and escape the loneliness that had been his constant companion since the inauguration. He simply did not know how, not without retreat.

Always a master at gauging Old Hickory's emotions, Martin Van Buren proposed an ingenious solution. He volunteered to resign from the cabinet, with the clear understanding that John Eaton would do likewise. The president would then be free to reorganize the council. Van Buren realized that he would be vacating a position traditionally occupied by the heir-apparent. Yet in his war against the "corrupt bargain," Jackson had altered the rules of the succession, declaring that he would not have the cabinet become a showcase for presidential aspirants. Van Buren shrewdly reasoned that he could do more to improve his standing with the president, and thus with the party, by appearing to relinquish power for the sake of unity. In fact there was little to relinquish. The New Yorker had never enjoyed great influence in the president's inner circle, where friendship and Western loyalties counted more heavily than the skills of the professional politician.

Jackson adopted the twin ideas of resignation and reorganization, but he was as emotional as Van Buren was deliberate. The President seemed unable to accept the stratagem merely as a convenience. The reform was essential to put down the "secrete workings of Duff Green, Calhoun and Co." who had recently published correspondence on the Seminole controversy and who had corrupted all the cabinet save Van Buren and Eaton. How the president looked forward to being rid of "the old *combination* of *gossips*—slanders, hypocrites, and false friends." Jackson's hatred of "Calhoun and Co." would have even greater impact on his decision to run for reelection and on his handling of the nullification crisis.

In his zeal to form a "united cabinet" Jackson threw consistency to the winds. His remarkable appointments, coupled with his apparent determination to consult the council on a regular basis, raised hopes that a bank compromise might be in the offing. Initially, Jackson wanted to appoint counselors who would help him check "the corrupting influence of the Bank upon the morals of the people and upon Congress." His final selections did more to cheer Nicholas Biddle than to energize the anti-Bank cause. Not one member of the new council was opposed to a recharter and two appointees, Secretary of State Edward Livingston and Secretary of the Treasury Louis McLane, were avowed friends of the Bank. McLane considered himself the architect of accord, quite obviously hoping that by arranging a settlement he could advance in the Democratic hierarchy. With Calhoun condemned and Van Buren taking up duties as minister to England, the enterprising secretary of the treasury felt confident that his services as a broker would outweigh the political insignificance of his native Delaware.

Jackson allowed the peace efforts to proceed for a variety of reasons. In the process of purging Calhoun's supporters, the president found release for some of the frustrations engendered by the Eaton affair. He looked upon his new cabinet as the harbinger of a more peaceful administration. Jackson was also calmed by the return of his nephew Andrew J. Donelson, who had been forced to leave the White House during the earlier stages of the Eaton affair. The reconciliation was on Jackson's terms. He saw himself as the injured father, the Donelsons as the wayward children, led astray by the forces of evil and corruption. Only their repentance would satisfy his injured pride and restore his sense of paternal authority. "I repeat the adage is true," Jackson lectured his nephew, " 'that a House Divided cannot stand.' " In his self-righteous determination to remove the division, Jackson applied the most cruel kinds of emotional pressure. "I am laboured almost to death, and have been a good deal afflicted; but will try amonghst strangers to get a man who will aid me and who will think it no disgrace to associate *with me and my friends.*" Donelson agreed to return as personal secretary and brought Emily back to Washington.

Jackson rejoiced at the restoration of order in his own family; he took further satisfaction from Nashville's polite reception of Peggy Eaton in the fall of 1831. "I am informed that fifty four of the members of the legislature (out of 69, the whole members, one being dead) attended the dinner, and that in the evening Eaton and his wife attended the Theatre which was crowded by an audience of the most fashionable and respectable." To complete this blissful scene Jackson proudly announced the approaching marriage of his adopted son to "the accomplished and said to be beautiful Miss York of Philadelphia"—unless there was "a slip between the cup and lip."

Total victory still seemed elusive. Although Jackson believed that "Duff Green, Calhoun and Co." would soon "be buried in the oblivion of forgetfulness for the profligate and wicked course they have pursued," he felt threatened by Calhoun's sinister methods. "All, *now*, who will not worship this idol are to be destroyed, or lyed down, if their intrigues can accomplish it?" Much as he longed to retire, Jackson could not rest while menaced by such men; he refused to "be driven" by his "enemies." Consequently he decided to run for reelection. The approaching campaign offered an excellent opportunity to achieve that ultimate public endorsement that slander and tragedy had palled in 1828. Calhoun remained enough of a threat to spark Jackson's anger, to arouse his energies, but not enough to make him worry unduly about losing the nomination. Nor did Henry Clay pose much of a challenge in the election itself. With the field relatively clear, Jackson looked forward to a contest in which the sole issue would be his own character and conduct. He anticipated an even greater margin of victory than he had received in 1828.

Biddle tried to capitalize on this new atmosphere of accord without comprehending its cause. He believed that Jackson was personally opposed to the Bank and once strengthened by reelection would never accept a recharter. Had he fully understood how much emotion Jackson had invested in the campaign, he might have realized that the president had no intention of letting issues interfere with his quest for personal vindication. If granted his precious mandate, Jackson was more likely to become the enthusiastic peacemaker than to remain the outraged warrior. As McLane once put it, Jackson would be "more disposed to yield when he is strong than when he is in danger."

Biddle compounded his error by assuming that the president was temporarily under the sway of his advisors and that they might break down Old Hickory's resistance to a recharter. Secretary of the Treasury McLane did very little to discourage this assumption. In October 1831, he met privately with Biddle and promised to exert whatever influence he could to obtain favorable mention of the Bank in Jackson's forthcoming message. McLane further stated that he intended to pursue an independent course in his own annual report. Biddle took heart at this meeting and no doubt reflected that the three thousands dollars he had loaned McLane's chief clerk was money well invested. With the appearance of the president's message and the secretary's report the compact seemed complete. "Having thus conscientiously discharged a constitutional duty," Jackson said of his previous criticism of the Bank, "I deem it proper on this occasion . . . to leave it for the present to an investigation of an enlightened people and their representatives." These mild remarks and McLane's recommendations for internal improvements, continuation of the tariff, and approval of a new charter convinced Biddle that the Bank's friends now ruled both the cabinet and the White House.

For the inconsistencies, vacillations, and confusion, Jackson had only himself to blame. On two previous occasions he had challenged the Bank's constitutionality without consulting his cabinet. He even went to the extreme of importing New York's James A. Hamilton to help draft both of these messages. Suddenly in December 1831, Hamilton was nowhere to be seen, the secretary of the treasury had resumed his normal responsibilities as the administration's chief fiscal spokesman, and Andrew Jackson was displaying uncharacteristic moderation on the Bank issue. Just as this change emboldened the president's political rivals, it dismayed some of his personal friends. "I am confined to my apartment living on asses milk and Sarsaparilla," wrote John Randolph of Roanoke, whose spirits took a turn for the worse after reading the annual message. "You are surrounded with evil counsellors," he cautioned Jackson; "you must find yourself in a false position."

The president appreciated the home remedies but not the political admonitions. "You will find Mr. McLane differs with me on the Bank," he retorted, "still it is an honest difference of opinion. Rest assured sir, Mr. McLane is a man of too much honor to play any game with me." Honorable or not, McLane was playing a game and Jackson knew nothing about it. The president claimed that the treasurer's report left him "free and uncommitted." Had he been aware of McLane's recent meeting with Biddle, Jackson might have taken Randolph's criticisms more to heart.

Biddle, too, was in a false position. He was under enormous pressure to petition for a recharter. Henry Clay, Daniel Webster, and other Bank supporters on Capitol Hill claimed they had the necessary votes for passage. Frustration fed their enthusiasm. For over three years, they had successfully thwarted almost all of the administration's legislative proposals, including the president's ill-fated recommendations on electoral reform and a government bank. Such obstructionism could not provide an adequate platform for opposing a candidate whose reputation had survived previous congressional setbacks. In the Bank, Clay and Webster saw an institution more powerful than the president and with nearly as many friends. The Bank and its branches boasted a system of communications equal to that of the Democratic party. The Kentuckian and his colleages concluded that if the election turned on the question of the Bank, many of Jackson's admirers would fall victim to conflicting loyalties. As the leading opposition candidate, Clay hoped to profit from this dilemma. Jackson's critics even welcomed the prospect of a presidential veto, believing that nothing could better highlight the growing threat of executive usurpation.

Like a lamb, Biddle lay down with the congressional lions. He steadfastly denied that politics dictated his decision to seek a recharter. He was bent on preserving the Bank and had merely relied on the advice of his experienced Washington friends as to the most propitious time for securing legislative approval. The Bank was his world, engaging all his energies, consuming his time, invading even the privacy of his country retreat. His fiscal correspondence alone was staggering; at times it must have seemed as though every one of the Bank's friends offered advice on how to proceed. These communications and the intense newspaper debates made detachment difficult. Biddle assumed that his friends shared his preoccupations, that they too put the best interests of the Bank ahead of personal profit or political gain. Somewhat naively, he placed his fate and that of the Bank in the hands of politicians whose main aim was to rescue the government from presidential excess. The alliance proved extremely effective in securing the passage of a recharter bill, but Biddle emerged from the congressional den shorn of much of his power.

The president could not remain free and uncommitted for very long. As soon as Biddle's allies introduced the recharter bill in early January 1832, such prominent Democratic papers as the *Richmond Enquirer* pledged Jackson to a veto. Francis P. Blair and Amos Kendall continued their journalistic war against the Bank through the columns of the *Washington Globe.* For the moment Jackson was silent, perhaps hoping that Congress might defeat the recharter as swiftly as it had dismissed his own recommendations for a government bank. He saw his enemies at work but did not consider their labor an immediate threat. "They know they cannot effect me," he reasoned. Rather, their aim was "to bring Calhoun or Clay into the presidency four years hence."

As the congressional session wore on, as the Senate rejected the nomination of Van Buren as minister to England, as a House committee investigated William B. Lewis's involvement in a land swindle, Jackson began to feel more vulnerable. Though he noted with satisfaction the unanimous Senate approval of a treaty with the Creek Indians, the president resented the criticism during debate. That Senators Clay and Calhoun had the audacity to quibble with the treaty illustrated "the malignity of these men. . . . They would if they could, overturn heavan and earth, to prostrate me. . . ." Physical ailments added to the president's increasing irascibility. "Our venerable patriot president has had a hard winter of it," Blair reported. "His wounded arm worried him, a set of artificial teeth has seemed to harrass him still more and our epidemic influenza wasted him considerably."

Democratic legislative strength seemed wasted as well. Despite their investigation of the Bank's charter violations, Thomas Hart Benton and other administration spokesmen were unable to stay Biddle's hand. The recharter bill passed the Senate early in June 1832 and seemed certain to receive the approval of the House. When members of his own party broke ranks to support the bill, Jackson saw the cabal once again. "The coalition are determined to press upon me at this session the bank," he told Van Buren. "I am prepared to meet them as I ought." Some influential Democrats thought the president ought to pursue a moderate course, to veto the bill if he must, but on grounds of prematurity, not constitutional principle. A mild veto, they reasoned, would leave the bill open for further debate, would allow the electorate to discuss the Bank fully during the canvass, and thus enable the new Congress to make more appropriate recommendations at the next session. Briefly, Jackson considered adopting such a course, but when the House passed the recharter bill early in July 1832, he abandoned moderation in favor of defiance.

The president took umbrage at reports that Biddle had charged him with seeking to purge the Bank of political dissidents. Jackson never could tolerate slander, especially when tinged with an element of truth. Such accusations convinced him that despite all Biddle's claims to the contrary, the Bank was a political monster, threatening the liberties of the people, but most of all bent upon destroying one Andrew Jackson. In expressing his fear, the President did not say, "The Bank is trying to kill the people" or "the party" or even "the presidency." "The Bank is trying to kill me": these were the fatal words. In vowing to resist, Jackson did not verbally recruit an army or even summon a second. "I will kill it," he said with singular determination.

With the passage of the recharter bill, the president knew there would be no way to keep the bank issue out of the election. If he followed the counsels of moderation he would only confuse the campaign by inviting the voters to discuss an issue as yet unresolved. Jackson desperately wanted vindication; the election had to turn on his conduct, not the Bank's misbehavior. Only an absolute veto that left no room for further negotiation would clear the way for such a contest. With the people asked to endorse the veto, rather than reject the recharter, Jackson might obtain his precious mandate.

On July 10, 1832, the president sent Congress a veto message clearly reflecting these personal motives. The words belonged to Amos Kendall and Roger B. Taney, the self-righteous indignation to Andrew Jackson. Instead of reciting the Bank's political sins, this triumvirate cast the entire message in the language of social apocalypse. The Bank was an engine of aristocracy, the symbol of special privilege, and the cause of the nation's discontent. Worse still, it was not even an indigenous monster, but rather the bastard offspring of American and European capitalism, ever susceptible to foreign influence. No matter that the Supreme Court had declared the Bank both national and constitutional. The president reserved for himself the right to interpret such matters; he invited the public to endorse his judgment. "I have now done my duty to my country," he said in closing. "If sustained by my fellow citizens, I shall be grateful and happy; if not, I shall find in the motives which impel me ample grounds for contentment and peace."

In issuing this veto and making himself equal to two-thirds of Congress, Jackson did not strengthen the presidency, nor did he intend to. He justified his veto on the grounds of state rights and limited government, forswearing any desire to augment executive prerogative. To him, the veto was a defensive weapon, a means of avoiding the excessive power that Congress would have him assume over internal improvements and the Bank. Granted, the threat of veto occasionally helped sway some votes in Congress, but few of Jackson's successors relished using the weapon since it raised anew the cry of executive usurpation. They preferred to manage legislative proceedings, not negate them. Each application of the veto power was a tacit admission of weakness, of failure to manipulate committees and marshal votes. This was a weakness that Jackson would be forced to admit more often than all his predecessors combined.

Far from being a prescription for enlarged executive authority, the Bank veto was a clever campaign document designed to simplify the issues. Democrats asked voters to choose between the forces of entrenched aristocracy and simple government, between a foreign dictatorship and a native American hero, between corruption and innocence—between the Bank and Andrew Jackson.

The choice proved more difficult than the president anticipated. Jackson won the election handily, receiving nearly 55 percent of the popular vote. He felt he deserved more. With the power of the government behind him, with opposition forces splintered, with the anti-Masons drawing off popular discontent, Jackson had expected to exceed his previous margin of victory. He was then, and remains now, the only president whose reelection to a second term was marred by a decline in popular approval. In part the results reflected public apathy. Proportionally fewer voters cast ballots in 1832 than in 1828. Reaction to the veto also cut into Jackson's margin, especially in Pennsylvania.

Denied a triumphant victory at the polls, the president nonetheless set out to play the role of conquering hero, willing to accept the support of all who would pledge personal fealty. He pushed the recharter fight from his mind and authorized overtures to men who six months before had been his staunchest opponents. Such tactics confounded many Democratic leaders who assumed that the party had found an issue at last, that once united against the Bank, Jacksonians would continue to wage war. They did not realize that the president was in fact preparing to fight a new enemy: not the hydra-headed monster of aristocratic monopoly but the serpent of disunion.

While creating confusion among Jackson's friends, the election of 1832 gave hope to his enemies. Previously weak and dispirited, the president's critics used the recharter fight to create the base for a new party. The veto served them well. Regardless of their feelings about Biddle's behavior or the Second Bank's utility, Henry Clay and his followers could unite to fight executive usurpation. This new opposition in Congress formed less than a month after the election and furthered the country's political turmoil.

As fate would have it, this confusion coincided with the most serious internal crisis in the young nation's history.

VII

"The Union Will Be Preserved"

NULLIFICATION: to Old Hickory's contemporaries it raised the frightening prospect of secession and civil war. "Good God! What do I behold?" cried General Winfield Scott, the man Jackson sent to South Carolina in anticipation of hostilities. "Impatient So. Carolina could not wait—she has taken a leap . . . when one member shall withdraw, the whole arch of union will tumble in." Despite years of agonizing debate and public discussion, the United States had never been able to agree on a theoretical definition of the Union. Yet the practical operation of government, the peaceful transfers of political power, the absence of revolutionary upheavals—all produced faith in the Union, however ill-defined. Nullification assaulted that faith.

In responding to nullification, the President followed no consistent political course, nor in the months ahead did he give much thought to the partisan consequences of his actions. Jackson believed that firmness alone would solve the crisis, that any temporizing would only encourage nullification and increase the threat of civil war. Reminiscent of his stance on the field of honor, the president's boldness proved a source of inspiration to many frightened Americans. At the same time, his determination and lack of flexibility jeopardized his party's efforts to arrange a political compromise.

Nullification stemmed from the unique structure of South Carolina's society. Nowhere else in the tidewater east did so few whites control so many blacks. The entrenched lowland rice culture, dominated by large plantation gang labor and absentee owners, set the tone for the state's political life. From their summer havens in Charleston, the plantation elite wined, dined, and entertained each other; the press of idle pleasures could not banish rumors of possible slave insurrections. The Denmark Vesey "conspiracy" in 1822 came as a rude reminder that despite the intricate system of badges, curfews, and codes, blacks remained a threat. If Vesey could conjure rebellion in Charleston, imagine what rebels might do among the black masses in the lowlands!

Economic instability heightened these growing apprehensions. With the Panic of 1819 and the abrupt end of the postwar economic prosperity, planters began to review their commitment to a system of national defenses and protective tariffs. This reappraisal coincided with the growing fear that the South was losing its control over the federal government and would therefore be unable to protect itself from abolitionist agitation and Northern hostility. The tariff soon became the symbol of South Carolina's discontent. From moderately high levels in 1816, duties on imported manufactured items nearly doubled by the time Andrew Jackson took office. With little industry to protect, South Carolina felt victimized by a Northern conspiracy. Other Southern states shared this feeling, but none prepared a remedy so drastic as nullification.

By 1832 the state had undergone a harrowing transformation from bastion of nationalistic fervor to outpost of secessionist sentiment. Much of the change related to the nature of South Carolina's peculiar institution. In October, while the rest of the nation was rendering its opinion of Andrew Jackson's attack on the Bank, South Carolina legislators took the momentous step of calling a state convention to implement the policy of minority veto. The move came after more than four years of intense soul-searching. Vice-president John C.

Calhoun had developed the theory of nullification, although he was reluctant to admit his authorship and even more reluctant to support theory with action. Based on the premise that sovereignty remained with the states and not the federal government, nullification involved the reactivation of the state convention, the institution that Calhoun and his colleagues believed had granted limited powers to the federal government by ratifying the Constitution. The state convention could guard against federal excess by judging for itself the constitutionality of congressional acts and declaring null and void those that violated the original grant of sovereignty. On November 24, 1832, South Carolina's state convention made just such a determination, announcing that it considered the tariff laws null and void and that in the event of federal coercion the state would secede.

Although he prided himself on being a South Carolinian "by birth," Andrew Jackson regarded this action as the work of madmen, not compatriots. Not that the president eschewed the role of plantation owner and slave master. Quite the contrary, ever since his adolescent visit to Charleston, Jackson had aspired to the life style of the tidewater aristocracy. Certainly the code of honor found no more ardent champion than the man who personally bore two bullets when he entered the White House. In the years immediately following the War of 1812, Jackson had realized his dream of building a comfortable estate. The Hermitage grew from a cluster of rude log cabins to a spacious brick dwelling that Jackson would eventually adorn with all the trappings of Southern gentility. He owned more than a section of land, given over to cultivation of cotton, corn, and oats. Nearly one hundred slaves lived in the cabins scattered across the fields. An additional forty blacks worked at his ward's estate in Alabama.

As a moderately wealthy planter, Jackson was immersed in the problems of slave management and control. He had great difficulty finding a reliable overseer for either the Alabama plantation or his own land. The constant search proved all the more annoying as ambition took him away from the Cumberland and forced him into the role of absentee owner. Jackson's prescriptions for care of his chattels differed little from those of other slave owners trying to turn a profit. "The increase of the Negroes is evidence of their health, & good treatment," he wrote his daughter-in-law in 1832. "I am happy to hear of it, as it will add to your wealth and that of your children." Attentive to the physical well-being of his slaves, Jackson was also careful to maintain discipline. In 1804 he advertised for a runaway slave, offering the finder additional reward for lashes laid on. Age did not soften Jackson's disciplinary instincts. When Rachel's maid began "putting on airs" and was judged "guilty of a great deal of impudence" Jackson "directed that the first impertinence she uses or the first disobedience of orders, that she will be publicly whipped." Instructions to a careless overseer best indicated the conflicting strains of paternalism and authoritarianism. "See Mr. Harris," Jackson wrote to John Coffee, "say to him to *rule, compel obedience,* but to extend as much kindness with this determination as circumstances will permit." Jackson was as suspicious as other slave masters; he, too, worried about the activities of "those itinerant yankies, who are endeavouring to poison the minds of our slaves."

Elevation to the presidency in no way reduced Jackson's activities as owner or anxieties as master. The campaign itself brought fresh charges that the Democratic candidate had once been a slave trader. Jackson reacted immediately, gathering evidence to refute his critics. He based his defense on a rather narrow definition, claiming that he had never bought blacks solely for the sake of speculation. Semantics aside, Jackson was involved in a number of transactions. In 1817, he sold Edward Livingston forty slaves valued at $24,000. During his two terms in the White House, Jackson continued to buy slaves for the Hermitage. On the eve of the nullification crisis, the president had the peculiar institution very much in mind. Late in the summer of 1832, before returning to Washington, Jackson dismissed his overseer for mismanagement. "He has injured me thousands and poisoned my servants with bad advice and conduct." The conduct troubled Jackson more than the waste. "I am sure Steel was worse than a drone to the hive."

Despite his suspicions of miscegenation and slave rebelliousness, despite his anguish over declining cotton prices, the president did not consider slavery on trial in the nullification crisis. The overwhelming predominance of black over white, so common in the lowlands of South Carolina, did not exist along the Cumberland. In 1832, blacks constituted no more than a quarter of the population of middle Tennessee. Personal animosities engendered by the Eaton affair combined with a strong attachment to the principle of Union determined Jackson's response to South Carolina's challenge far more than any concern over slavery or economics.

The Jackson administration and the state of South Carolina became opponents after more than two years of political friendship. The nullifiers (or "nullies" as the president called them) supported the Democratic campaign in 1828, hoping that victory would lead to immediate downward revision of the tariff. Jackson did very little to inspire this expectation, issuing bland statements on the tariff calculated to appeal to a wide variety of economic and sectional interests. Yet with the president in such delicate health and the author of nullification occupying the vice-presidency, prospects for compromise looked better than at any time since the fall of the Virginia Dynasty. The Eaton affair soon dispelled this naive optimism.

"It would have been better for the President to have left Mrs. E. to stand or fall on her own merits," observed one of Jackson's Tennessee friends at the end of the crisis, "& not to have made her the test by which he tries his friends." The president's reaction to this affair, more than any ideological or political animosity, caused Calhoun's downfall. Once Jackson saw the vice-president's wife in the vanguard of Peggy Eaton's

critics, he was finally willing to believe all the rumors that
Calhoun had been his chief detractor during the Monroe administration's deliberations on the Seminole War. "You know
the confidence I once had in that Gentleman," Jackson wrote
in December 1829. With that confidence waning and "that
Gentleman" so conspicuous a member of "a corrupt and *profligate* community," the president began to blame all of his
"troubles vexations and difficulties" on "Mr. Calhoun and
some of his friends."

Ironically, the public caught its first glimpse of the conflict
in April 1830 at a dinner celebrating Democratic unity. The
president read the list of prepared toasts and immediately
"saw the whole plot." Only the most intensely suspicious mind
could divine a nullification conspiracy from the accumulated
verbiage of twenty-four protracted pledges of state-rights doctrine. Jackson limited his own reponse to those now famous
seven words: "Our Federal Union—It must be preserved." In
making this historic declaration, the president did not intend
to commit himself or his party to a new ideological course. By
his own account, he thought of the toast on the spur of the
moment; characteristically, he rushed to the offensive.

Had his audience been in a more philosophical mood, had
they been less under the influence of the preceding toasts, they
might have detected what subsequent, sober scholars have
found: a bold deviation from state-rights orthodoxy. Adams,
Hamilton, or Webster might have made such an offering, although each would have expanded it eloquently. They did not;
Andrew Jackson did. The president believed the nullifiers
needed proof of executive determination, not a lesson in constitutional philosophy. And so he stared directly at Calhoun
while delivering his statement. Like so many of his impulsive
attacks, this sally succeeded brilliantly. Calhoun was caught off
guard. He tried to return Jackson's steely gaze, but his ner-
vousness betrayed him. His hand trembled ever so slightly as
Jackson spoke, sending "a little of the amber fluid" trickling
down the side of his glass.

Prepared though he was for any kind of philosophical dispu-
tation, the vice-president simply did not know how to deal with
Jackson's overt hostility. He made the mistake of underesti-
mating the president's outrage and assuming it was mere political contrivance. Worse still, Calhoun saw Van Buren as the
evil counselor leading the monarch astray. In December 1830,
when he received an invitation to dine at the White House,
Calhoun eagerly became the faithful courtier come to rid the
palace of villainy. He decided to clear the air once and for all
by publishing all his correspondence on the Seminole affair,
plus an additional exposé of Van Buren's machinations in the
Eaton scandal. The vice-president saw this publication as a
monument to honesty.

Jackson deeply resented publication of court secrets. The
Seminole controversy raked over in Calhoun's pamphlet
seemed least important; having defended himself on this matter before, Jackson was ready to do so again. He reserved his
special anger for those letters dealing with the Eaton affair.
For nearly two years the president had struggled to assert his
authority over his cabinet and over his family, to teach both a
sense of social propriety. Calhoun held all these efforts up for
public inspection, inviting the ridicule of uninformed journal-
ists and, worse yet, more debate about Peggy Eaton's character. At first Jackson thought of responding to Calhoun, of
confining the reply solely to military matters in the hope of
diverting attention from Mrs. Eaton. He soon abandoned the
idea after such friendly papers as the *Richmond Enquirer* regis-
tered their dismay over Washington's petticoat politics. Finally
Van Buren stepped forward with the plan to restructure the
cabinet and remove Eaton from the center of public attention.

Never before had Jackson found such willing scapegoats; as
he so indelicately put it: "Duff Green, Calhoun and Co." had
"cut their own throats." Firmly believing that the vice-president had committed political suicide, Jackson felt absolved
from any guilt in the purge that passed under the name of
cabinet reorganization. Calhoun alone would have to bear the

blame for disrupting the council and bringing about the down-fall of his own supporters. In the process of constructing this defense, Jackson also blamed his vice-president for the "man-ner and secrete plans of the junto, with members of Con-gress," that produced "opposition to my measures recommended and particularly to the bill for removal of the Indian." Even though this act had passed into law nearly a year before, Jackson still resented its critics. Men who would stand in the way of Indian removal while attacking a virtuous woman for political advantage were not men at all but mere "puppits." They deserved to be removed from office where "Everyone stripped of his covering will have to fight under his own co-lours, and not under the strength of others. . . . The people will judge them by their fruit."

In forming a new cabinet, the president displayed as much ideological as fiscal inconsistency. Barely a year before he had reaffirmed his support of state rights in the Maysville veto; yet in the summer of 1831, he appointed Louis McLane and Ed-ward Livingston to the most important cabinet posts. The two new secretaries were Bank supporters and former Federalists with little devotion to the doctrines of strict construction and limited government. Jackson freely admitted these partisan deviations. "He is a polished scholar, an able writer, and a most excellent man," the president said of Livingston, "but he knows nothing of mankind." Jackson was willing to tolerate a "little Federal leavan" simply because the two Federalists in question were loyal and would not undermine cabinet har-mony. In sum: none of his new counselors wore Calhoun's "colours."

The personal animosity between the nation's two highest elected officials reached a new level of intensity shortly after Congress convened in December 1831. In an emotionally charged scene on the floor of the Senate, Calhoun cast the deciding vote against confirmation of Van Buren as minister to England. "It will kill him, sir, kill him dead," the vice-president exultantly shouted. "He will never kick, sir, never kick." The president flew into a towering rage at these trumped-up proceedings. Furiously, he wrote letters denouncing Calhoun as "one of the most base hypocritical and unprincipled villains in the United States" and claiming that the Senate vote was a "wanton act" that "degraded that August body" and made it an international disgrace more heinous even "than the Spanish inquisition." Like so many outraged Democrats, Jackson immediately predicted that the Senate rejection would redound to Van Buren's favor and make him the next vice-president.

Both political and personal considerations prompted Jackson's instant endorsement of his former secretary of state. Senate rejection reinforced the image of Van Buren as selfless statesman, willing to relinquish power and prestige for the sake of party unity. This picture of the victimized public servant neatly complemented the portrait of the embattled chief executive still at war with the forces of corruption. For the moment this shade of self-sacrifice covered the personal disagreements between the two men. Jackson saw more than political advantage in Van Buren's nomination for vice-president; he also glimpsed a golden opportunity for revenge. What more fitting way to punish Calhoun's hypocrisy, to leave him "naked to the world," than to place Van Buren "in the chair of the very man whose casting vote rejected you." Jackson craved this delicious irony. The Senate action had been more than an assault on "our national character"; it was an "insult offered to the Executive" as well. Jackson had never been a man to take insult lightly.

The president's feud with Calhoun all but destroyed effective communications with South Carolina; failure to achieve significant tariff reform further aggravated the situation. Before the opening of the congressional session in December 1831, Jackson talked optimistically about his forthcoming recommendations to lower duties and thereby "annihilate the nullifiers as they will be left without any pretext of Complaint." The president was a reluctant convert to such compromise,

, that the nullifiers were intent on "disunion" and
ve only indulged in their vituperations against the Tariff
for the purpose of covertly accomplishing their ends." Jackson's suspicions, coupled with the administration's preoccupation with the Bank's recharter, help explain the outcome of the 1832 tariff debates. Congress rejected Louis McLane's recommendations, instead adopting a bill sponsored by John Quincy Adams. Overall tariff rates declined but the crucial levies on iron, cotton, and woolens remained the same. The nullifiers still had persuasive evidence of a Northern conspiracy. Jackson recognized the continuing clamor but attributed it to "disappointed ambition, orginating with unprincipled men who would rather rule in hell, than be subordinate in heavan."

When the election of 1832 prevented Democrats from taking command of Congress and denied Jackson his cherished mandate, he searched for a way to subordinate these hellish "demagogues." Jackson's powerful lieutenant, Amos Kendall, wrote to Martin Van Buren suggesting a new alliance between the Democrats and the defeated supporters of Henry Clay. "By prompt attention to these men," the party could "secure a majority of the Senate at the coming session." Kendall further argued that such an entente would enable supporters "of all parties in the Northern, middle and Western States" to stand united against nullification. Quite clearly, Kendall wanted to build a coalition in Congress capable of defeating South Carolina and serving as the nucleus for a new national party. To do so he was willing to divert attention from the Bank and abandon the traditional North–South axis of the Jackson alliance.

As architect and theorist of the alliance, Van Buren was deeply troubled. To him orthodoxy and discipline were precious commodities, especially in a crisis. The vice-president-elect curtly reminded Kendall that the Democratic alliance had always been opposed to amalgamation, that compacts with the likes of Henry Clay would undermine discipline and destroy the party's commitment to state rights. Such a dramatic shift in political focus would alienate the South and invite sectional discord. Kendall retreated a step or two, explaining that he had not intended to suggest a total fusion of Democrats and Clayites. "We must not court them nor meet their advances. The effect of either, as you remark, would be to strengthen the Nullifiers of the South." Still, Kendall wanted some "moral force" to be "arrayed on the side of the administration" to combat "the incipient treason of the South." He closed with a crude threat. "At this moment I look upon you as the rallying point of the republican party; but events of a few years may make it necessary . . . that its favor shall be bestowed upon another."

Surely Kendall would not have undertaken such correspondence on his own initiative. As a result of the Bank War he had emerged as the president's closest official confidant, author of the veto message, soon to become the architect of the deposit banking system. "He is supposed to be the moving spring of the whole administration, the thinker, the planner, and doer," Harriet Martineau informed her British readers several years later. "But it is all in the dark." All, that is, save the innumerable conferences with Andrew Jackson where the two made major decisions on a wide range of fiscal and political problems.

Van Buren might have reacted differently had the suggestion of party reorganization come from any other member of the administration. Francis P. Blair was noted for irresponsible statements; McLane, Livingston, and Cass served the president faithfully without enlisting his private admiration. The other cabinet members stood on the periphery of power. Only Kendall, Donelson, and Lewis had constant access to Jackson's private plans. Knowing this, Van Buren replied promptly, couching his rebuttal in the strongest possible terms in the hope of reaching the president.

As Congress assembled in early December 1832, the president seemed publicly unperturbed by the "incipient treason of the South." He promised to "pass it barely in review as a mere buble." In his annual message he recommended further tariff reductions, hoping that they might remove South Carolina's cause for complaint. Privately, Jackson was a good deal more exercised, saying of nullification, "It leads directly to civil war and bloodshed and deserves the execration of every friend of the country." When the "buble" burst, Jackson exploded. "The Nullifiers of the South has *run mad,*" he said after hearing that South Carolina's convention had adopted the nullification ordinance. Instead of delaying his annual message, Jackson let his conciliatory gestures stand and hurriedly began to prepare a special appeal to the American people.

Andrew Jackson approached the nullification crisis with the determination of a crusader who had finally found the ultimate cause. Again and again he declared *"the Union will be preserved,"* as if the word *Union* itself had mystical properties. Like many other troubled Americans, Jackson took refuge in a historic concept that had defied definition but had powerful emotional appeal. Its invocation alone was enough to create a common bond of patriotic sentiment. In a decentralized society incapable of developing effective communications and lacking strong national institutions, such symbols served a crucial function. They helped foster a feeling of nationalism. For Jackson the Union had additional, more personal significance. Since adolescence he had dreaded disorder. In Indian relations, in politics, in the social life of the Washington community he had felt himself threatened by impending chaos and had sought relief by asserting his authority in an attempt to restore order.

The president conceived of the Union as the highest form of social order—the family writ large on a national scale. Just as he had desperately tried to preserve his personal and official families during the Eaton affair, so he would now struggle with equal fervor to maintain the Union. Calhoun remained the enemy; Jackson easily transferred all his old hatreds and prejudices to the new crusade. Unionists in South Carolina facilitated the transfer by feeding Jackson's suspicions. "The principle object of these unprincipled men," wrote unionist leader Joel R. Poinsett, was "to embarrass your administration and defeat your election; but they have led the people on so far under other pretexts."

The president totally rejected nullification as a legitimate form of political action. Any man who would preach disunion was not only evil, he was insane. "The wickedness, the madness and folly of the leaders and the delusion of their followers in the attempt to destroy themselves and our Union has not its paralel in the history of the world," Jackson proclaimed. The president believed that the nullifiers had "run mad," that they were intent on the ultimate insanity: a "Southern confederacy," a political Hades where ambition, intrigue, and demagoguery would reign supreme. "The tariff was only the pretext," he argued later. "The next pretext will be the Negro, or slavery question."

Jackson did not quaver at the thought of using force to subdue this madness or at the thought that force might bring civil war. The nullifiers had tried to prevent his reelection and now were challenging the Union. Compromise would do little good. It would only encourage them. The time for discussion had passed; the time for action had come. Jackson would meet nullification as he had met previous challenges, with determination to defend himself and his principles. He fully recognized the risk. "I will die with the Union," he said fearlessly.

In preparing his nullification proclamation, Andrew Jackson literally perceived himself as a father charged with the responsibility of leading his errant children back from the edge of the abyss. He wrote a rough draft of the message himself, then turned it over to Edward Livingston for translation into appropriate nationalistic entreaties. Jackson did insist on a personal statement "for the conclusion of the Proclamation." "Seduced as you have been my fellow countrymen by the delusive theories and misrepresentations of ambitious, deluded and designing men, I call upon you, in the language of truth and with the feelings of a father to retrace your steps." In the final message, the blunt language disappeared but the paternalistic persuasions remained—a reminder to the attentive that for Andrew Jackson this was both a personal and a constitutional crisis.

The president refused to dilute his own response with political artifice. All of the conciliation evident in the annual message disappeared in his proclamation of December 10, 1832. "I, Andrew Jackson, President of the United States," the paper began, "have thought it proper to issue this my proclamation. . . ." Had he followed this formal opening with a general appeal to the concept of Union, "had the proclamation been as empty and inflated as a balloon," as one stalwart Democrat put it, it might have "carried through the Union with applause." Instead, Jackson insisted on "stating my views of the constitution." Point by point, the proclamation refuted the theory of nullification, even to the extent of extended discourse on the nature of the Union. "The Constitution of the United States, then, forms a government not a league," the president declared. "It is a government in which all the people are represented, which operates directly on the people as individuals, not on the States." This was no casual evaluation of the federal compact, but a dramatic deviation from state-rights doctrine. When asked if he might eliminate such sentiments for the sake of party harmony, Jackson replied, "Those are my views and I will not change them nor strike them out." He was determined to have the country accept his political philosophy and thereby reject the preachments of Calhoun. To do so, he had to draw the ideological battle lines as clearly as possible. To show respect for the doctrines of state rights might seem a mark of weakness.

In this proclamation, the president seemed bent on summoning the very "moral force" of which Kendall spoke, the force that made Van Buren fear the wholesale loss of Southern support. Jackson's insistence on definition, his bold constitutional statements, placed loyal state-rights Democrats like Thomas Ritchie in an extremely uncomfortable position. Although he admired the patriotic tone of the message and agreed that nullification was unwise and premature, Ritchie's *Richmond Enquirer* mentioned "some *doctrinal points, . . .* to which we think it our duty to state we cannot subscribe. They are not essentially connected with the main object of the Proclamation," he assured his readers. But then he continued, "These doctrines relate to the *right* of secession—and to the *character* of the federal compact." Had they been written with tongue in cheek such editorial evasions might have added comic relief to the crisis. State-rights theory was no laughing matter, not to Thomas Ritchie at least. For the moment he controlled his disgust: "May the voice of the father be listened to with the respect it deserves." Administration critics listened to the voice, read the tortured rationalizations of loyal editors like Ritchie, and then burst into rejoicing at the Democratic dilemma. "The effect was electric," wrote one Virginia nullifier. "General Gordon and Mr. Tyler . . . Both sprang up, caught each other in their arms and danced around the room like children in a delirium of joy." While the "children" danced, the "father" prepared to support his "moral force" with martial might.

From the moment he heard of the nullification ordinance, Jackson concentrated all his energies on making an appropriate military response. He said no more about tariff reduction as a basis for compromise. Early in 1833, administration spokesmen introduced a bill to lower rates, but there is little indication that Jackson lent his support. He was too busy with his duties as commander-in-chief.

Ironically, Jackson's military experience complicated preparations. As a battlefield commander he had rarely been involved in administrative matters, nor had he learned to delegate authority. When it came time to establish communications with unionist leaders in Charleston, Jackson personally attended to the details of reinforcement, supply, troop movements, and naval support. In November 1832, he dispatched General Winfield Scott to Charleston, ostensibly to inspect federal garrisons at Ft. Moultrie and Castle Pinckney, but in reality to make a minor show of military strength. Yet he allowed Scott little leeway. Nor did Secretary of War Lewis Cass have much control over preparations. "Cass is an amiable and talented man, a fine writer," Jackson once remarked, "but unfortunately it is hard for him to say no and he thinks all men honest." Never prone to trust any man, Jackson considered Cass's credulity a sign of weakness. He wanted no weak men around him during the confrontation with South Carolina.

Instead of working through the secretary of war, Jackson opened a personal correspondence with the head of the unionist forces in Charleston, Joel R. Poinsett. A former minister to Mexico whose rashness had led to a presidential recall, Poinsett immediately ingratiated himself with Jackson by denouncing Calhoun's supporters as a corrupt oligarchy and contending that their real object was to injure Jackson personally. At the outset of the crisis, both men prepared for hostilities. Poinsett asked the president for a hundred rifles; Jackson sent five thousand. Poinsett spoke of the need for federal troops; Jackson replied that "in forty days I can have within the limits of So. Carolina fifty thousand men, and in forty days more another fifty thousand." Rumors circulated that Jackson intended to lead the army himself, that he had summoned John Coffee to Washington to be his second in command. As one critic put it: "Jackson pants for the sword."

The president may well have dreamed of one final military adventure, but he was all too familiar with the hazards of raising an army. Without some overt act by the nullifiers he could not mobilize federal troops or call upon the state militia. Any precipitous move by the government would not only make recruitment difficult, it would further alienate South Carolina's neighbors and increase the likelihood that they too might endorse nullification. Jackson therefore agreed with Poinsett that the unionists in Charleston should only draw arms "for self protection and in the defence of the laws."

Still, the administration's initial strategy was provocative. Jackson knew full well that the nullifiers intended to raise troops for their own defense. He vowed "to meet such action at the threshold," to brand it as sedition, and to "have the leaders arrested and arrayed for treason." Van Buren and other party leaders were aghast at such a bold strategy. From Albany the vice-president-elect urged Jackson to reconsider his definition of treason, "to decide whether the *mere passage* of the bills would constitute the crime and justify the measures you speak of." Eventually Jackson adopted a different approach: he would await word that the nullifiers were "in hostile array in opposition to the execution of the laws" before making arrests and authorizing the use of federal troops. The change of heart came as the result of military necessity, not the councils of moderation. By mid-January 1833, the president learned that the unionists would not join in a marshall's posse to arrest their fellow South Carolinians but would only shoulder arms under direct order from the federal government. In short, Poinsett was afraid of becoming a party to provocation.

While the president was preoccupied with these military matters, his counselors worked behind the scenes to effect a compromise. Lewis Cass tried to repair relations with Virginia, even publishing an unsigned letter in the *Richmond Enquirer*, urging the Old Dominion to send a peace delegation to South Carolina. Although the Junto accepted the advice, Ritchie remained dubious of Jackson's intentions. Louis McLane corresponded with customs collectors in Charleston and developed a procedure for receiving duties at the federal forts in the harbor rather than in the city itself. This transfer reduced the chances of armed assault on government agents. Jackson later received credit for this peaceful tactic, although the original plan came from Poinsett.

By far the most concerted administration peace effort began shortly after Congress convened. New York Congressman Gulian Verplanck, suddenly elevated to the chairmanship of the House Ways and Means Committee, introduced a new tariff bill early in January 1833. Drafted largely by Louis McLane and James K. Polk, the measure called for a general reduction of duties over the next year. The *Washington Globe* endorsed the bill and Van Buren carefully shepherded his congressional friends into the reductionist camp. Two obstacles stood in the way of quick passage: lack of Democratic party discipline and the president's warlike intentions.

During his first term of office, Andrew Jackson fought with the Congress over appointments, public policy, even social etiquette. Aside from the Indian removal act, he failed to win approval of measures that he considered vital to the country's welfare, such as electoral reform and rotation in office. The most famous accomplishments of his first term were executive vetoes, acts necessitated by a lack of party unity. In 1833, congressional Democrats were so divided that they could not even elect Francis P. Blair as congressional printer. "Although I have been reelected by an overwhelming majority," Jackson lamented, "Congress has elected Gales and Seaton printers to the House of Representatives, and Green for the Senate, so you see Congress pays Gales and Seaton for abusing me the last twelve years, and Duff Green for the last three."

Had the President been able to suppress such pique, had he come out strongly in favor of tariff reform, had he rallied Democratic forces on Capitol Hill, he might have been able to rescue the Verplanck bill. Andrew Jackson did none of these things. In his view tariff reform was a chimera. "No my friend," he responded to Van Buren's pleas for moderation, "the crisis must be met with firmness, our citizens protected and the modern doctrine of nullification and secession put down forever." The president actually worried "whether some of the eastern states may not secede or nullify, if the tariff is reduced. I have to look at both ends of the union to preserve it." Jackson intended to "appeal to Congress," not for compromise, but for more power to arrest "those who may commit treasonable acts." On January 16, 1833, the president sent Congress his famous "force bill" message.

To a community already buffeted by rumors of imminent civil war, the president's message came as a biting northern wind, driving and relentless. For the second time in a little over a month, he denounced the theory of nullification and expressed his determination to uphold the laws. To execute his responsibilities more efficiently, he requested modifications in the procedure of customs collecting. Jackson also asked Congress to empower the federal judiciary to try cases if the South Carolina courts proved recalcitrant. Taken by themselves these appeals were quite innocuous. Placed in the context of the remainder of the message, they assume more ominous significance. In the opening paragraphs of the message, Jackson branded South Carolina the aggressor, claiming that its forces were already "in the attitude of hostile preparation" and were bent, "on military violence if need be to enforce her laws." He assumed that the nullifiers were determined to carry out their threat of challenging federal statutes. By removing some of the administrative and legal loopholes that had hitherto offered them nonviolent methods of resistance, Jackson hoped to place their aggression in the clearest possible light. In sum, Jackson was convinced that fighting would erupt; before that happened he wanted Congress to place the law clearly on his side.

In military terms, the force-bill message was more important for what it did not say. Jackson made no request for broader powers, for contingency funds, for specific strategic reprisals, as he would later in the Mexican claims dispute. He simply stated his intention to meet force with force, confident that existing federal laws would cover his actions as commander-in-chief. Privately, he told Poinsett that if pressed he would summon troops even "if Congress fail to act on the bill."

Since the president requested only minor statutory modifications and was fully prepared to proceed on his own, why did he send such an emphatic message to Congress? "It was my duty to make known to Congress the state of the Union," Jackson explained at the time. Duty may have prompted the report but experience gave it substance. Jackson despaired of any congressional solution to the nullification crisis. In his

view Congress harbored a group of willful politicians concerned only with individual aggrandizement and not with solv-
ing the nation's problems. He sensed that his own followers
were not strong enough to carry the Verplanck bill. Jackson
would accept support from the opposition, but only on his own
terms. He would not stoop to bargain with the cabal. Such
bargaining might only elevate Calhoun and encourage the
nullifiers to prolong their rebellion. Nor did the president
have the time or the inclination to build a loyal congressional
following, not in the midst of a crisis, not when military matters commanded so much of his time.

Yet Jackson wanted to array the central government under
his banner. He had to show that the entire Washington community denounced nullification and stood ready to back his
use of force. By asking for very little, by preceding his request
with a lengthy constitutional discourse, by referring to his own
power as commander-in-chief, Jackson hoped to win endorsement for his unionist doctrines as well as for his military authority.

The president's failure to recommend compromise, his insistence on confrontation, killed any lingering hope of passing
the Verplanck tariff. Democrats and National Republicans
alike began to share Daniel Webster's conclusion that Jackson
preferred "the individual honor of suppressing nullification
now" and taking "his own time hereafter to remodel the
tariff." With the president pursuing one course and his adherents another, Democrats lost all control over the legislature.
Jackson's archenemy Henry Clay took advantage of this
predicament to rush forward his own tariff bill. Clay immediately enlisted Calhoun's support; the vice-president had resigned after the election so that he might return to his old seat
in the Senate. Predictably, Jackson blamed the South
Carolinian for the failure of the Verplanck bill. By mid-February 1833, Clay's tariff proposal was gathering support, most
notably from Democrats who had already read in the annual
message that reduction of duties would help resolve the crisis.

Jackson only contributed to these defections by allowing his earlier statements to stand uncorrected.

As Clay maneuvered toward compromise, Jackson began to feel a deep sense of personal injury. Congress appeared insensitive to the military situation in South Carolina. It ignored his warnings and seemingly scoffed at his suggestions that firmness alone would save the Union. After hearing that Clay's tariff proposal might actually take precedence over the force bill, Jackson raged at Tennessee Senator Felix Grundy:

> Surely you and my friends will rush that bill thro' the Senate. . . . This is due to the Country—it is due to me, and to the safety of this Union and surely you and others of the committee who reported it will never let it slumber one day until it passes the Senate. Lay *all* delicacy on this subject aside and compell every man's name to appear upon the journals that the nullifiers may *all* be distinguished from those who are in support of the laws, and the Union.

Opposition forces in Congress let Jackson have his way. Early in March 1833, Congress passed the force bill and immediately thereafter the compromise tariff. For South Carolina and for the nation, the lowering of the duties ended the crisis. The president considered the resolution shaky at best. He still thought the nullifiers would reactivate their protest and that some military force might be necessary to restrain them. Preoccupation with this possibility protected him from a fact obvious to most of his contemporaries: Henry Clay had arranged the compromise. Jackson never conceded the importance of tariff reform, certainly not one arranged by the arch-intriguer whose earlier bargains had been so corrupt.

Nor did the president admit the political consequences of his show of force. By failing to support the Verplanck bill, he undermined the credibility of his counselors who continued to support his earlier contention that tariff reform would leave the nullifiers with little cause for complaint. He alienated his vice-president and heir-apparent; ambition alone kept Van Buren from registering his dismay more forcefully. Worse still,

Jackson injured the Southern wing of the Democratic party by his repeated refusal to distinguish between legitimate adherence to state rights and illegitimate advocacy of nullification. Kendall's bold talk of restructuring the party and the president's own flirtations with Daniel Webster had prompted considerable speculation that Jackson was preparing a major realignment of the coalition. The nullification proclamation and the force-bill message gave substance to these rumors, creating wholesale defections in Virginia and North Carolina. These, along with the growing opposition to executive usurpation, gave momentum to the fledgling Whig party that would soon challenge Democratic supremacy, first in the South and then throughout the country.

If Jackson recognized these realities, he chose to ignore them. In his view state politicians had little appreciation for the nature of the nullification crisis. They worried about ideological trifles while he faced the prospect of martial rebellion. He wanted their support not their suspicions. "Why is your legislature so silent," he angrily asked Van Buren at the height of the controversy. Like many other party leaders, the New Yorker could only shake his head in dismay.

Democrats did not expect Andrew Jackson to provide such vigorous executive leadership. The party drew its strength from the cooperation of state political organizations. Commitment to the ideology of state rights helped maintain this cooperative spirit; placing limitations on the power of the central government in turn protected and encouraged state sovereignty and activism. By word, by deed, Andrew Jackson undermined this commitment, thereby raising doubts about his own devotion to maintain the Democratic coalition. While applauding the salvation of the Union, many of his supporters feared the destruction of the party.

VIII

Hail and Farewell

THE OPPORTUNITY was irresistible. His confidence shaken by the revolt in Congress, his health once again in delicate condition, the president looked forward to escaping the capital for "a change of air and relaxation from business." This would prove no ordinary vacation. Early in June 1833, accompanied by a large retinue of dignitaries, Jackson began a tour of the East from Baltimore to Boston. Twelve miles outside the Maryland metropolis, Andrew Jackson left his carriage and boarded the steam cars of the Baltimore and Ohio Railroad, thus becoming the first president to travel by train. This symbolic event escaped all but the most casual notice. Jackson's thoughts turned to the warm glow of the revolutionary past, not to the jarring prospects of the technological future. Like Washington and Monroe before him, the president embarked on a grand tour to bring the presidency to the people. Some Democratic spokesmen, especially those unaware of the trip's psychological dimension, worried that Jackson was setting out to restructure the coalition. In the parades and the unprecedented ovations, they saw the makings of a new political engine that might batter down the traditional pillars of the Democratic party.

Newspapers dubbed the prospective alliance a Constitution and Union party. According to their predictions, the president had come east to join forces with "The Godlike" Daniel Webster. Together the Old Hero and the stentorian statesman

would continue their war against disunion. Events of the nullification winter had lent substance to these rumors. No sooner
had Kendall announced the search for new allies, than Jackson
abandoned state rights in his proclamation. Webster heartily
approved the shift in principles; during debate on the tariff
and force bills, he consistently came to the administration's
aid. Jackson in turn thanked Senator Webster and accepted the
Massachusetts legislature's invitation to visit New England after Congress adjourned.

As the tour progressed, Jackson seemed disposed to bury
old partisan animosities. The public adulation exceeded his
wildest dreams. Weary but exhilarated by the exhausting
round of receptions in New York City, he wrote to his son, "I
have bowed to upwards of two hundred thousand people to-
day—never has there been such affection of the people before
I am sure been evinced. Party has not been seen here." Jackson
cherished this affection and doggedly subjected himself to a
murderous schedule of parades, banquets, and ceremonies.
Weaving its way across Connecticut to the accompaniment of
thunderous bursts of cannon fire, the presidential entourage
finally reached Boston. For four days the city lavished affection
on the Old Hero; Harvard College awarded him an honorary
law degree. John Quincy Adams refused to witness his alma
mater's "disgrace in conferring her highest literary honors
upon a barbarian who could not write a sentence of grammar
and hardly could spell his own name." Perverse though it may
have been, Jackson took pleasure in these proceedings, as he
did in the sight of the thousands of Bostonians who lined the
streets whenever his carriage passed. For the heart-warming
reception, Jackson had Daniel Webster to thank; the senator
had carefully arranged that New England put her best face
forward.

While Jackson marched ceremoniously across the northeast-
ern countryside, his prospective ally assayed political fortunes
in the West. Starting at Albany, and proceeding to Cincinnati,

Webster held a series of conferences with Democratic leaders and reiterated his support for the president's forceful handling of the nullification crisis. For the moment, he stopped short of advocating creation of a new party, fearful no doubt of alienating Henry Clay and other National Republicans whose friendship he still valued. Like Jackson's junket, Webster's tour kept the rumor mills working overtime. Newspaper editorials heralded an end to old party distinctions: "Let us have no Jacksonians nor National Republicans, . . . no Free Masons nor Anti-Masons nor Southrons or Northmen but let all be for the principles of the Proclamation, and let the watchword be Union and the Constitution."

Much as the prospect of a party rallying around the proclamation appealed to the president's injured pride, a Jackson–Webster coalition was not in the stars. Not that the president was ideologically opposed to alliance with Federalists; the two men were simply incompatible. Jackson's habitual suspicions stood in the way of new friendships. "I have said before and now repeat, the world is not to be trusted." Jackson trusted only Westerners: Kendall, Lewis, Overton, Coffee, and Donelson. Travel though he might, Webster could not discard his New England heritage. Van Buren had managed to overcome such provincial prejudices but only after years of self-effacing labor and with considerable sacrifice of personal integrity. A master at judging Jackson's temper, the vice-president had learned when to advance, when to retreat, and when to stay safely out of harm's way. The "Godlike Daniel" was a public man, accustomed to measuring his own worth in terms of popular esteem. Jackson wanted no such rival for either democratic or providential favor.

Ultimately an old enemy killed the new friendship. Jackson had been willing to set aside party to combat disunion. Once the nullification crisis was over, he returned to attack the Bank with renewed vigor. He blamed the monster for his congressional troubles, especially for the corrupt "coalition between Clay and Calhoun" that produced the compromise tariff. "This combination wields the U. States Bank and with its corrupting influence they calculate to carry everything," he maintained. Citing Biddle's huge press subsidies and extensive loans to congressmen, Jackson believed the "liberty of the country" was in jeopardy. He vowed never to retire "until I can strangle that hydra of corruption." Daniel Webster could explain away a decade of doctrinal differences, but not his retainer from the Second Bank of the United States.

Additional, more personal reasons prompted the president to renew his crusade against the Bank. While he was struggling so hard to preserve the Union, his own family was beginning to fall into disarray. Rumors reached him that his overseer was mistreating the slaves and that several had died as a consequence. Jackson dispatched William B. Lewis to make a thorough investigation of the charges and to report on conditions at the Hermitage. Normally such duties would have fallen to the president's adopted son, but Andrew Jackson, Jr., was proving an inept plantation manager. The Hermitage burned in 1834; Jackson could barely conceal his disgust. He invoked the usual providential rationalizations, but privately suspected that his son's negligence led to the disaster.

Death further weakened family bonds. In the spring of 1833, John Overton died, depriving Jackson of his oldest political confidant. Less than six months later, John Coffee succumbed following a brief illness. "A better or braver man never existed," Jackson extolled, "and I mourn his loss with the feelings of David for his son Jonathan." Mourning was too painful; in the next breath Jackson said, "It is useless to mourn, he is gone the way of the earth, and I will soon follow him." This was no idle statement. Since early spring, Jackson had been suffering from headaches, chest pains, fevers, and bowel disturbances. Four years of incessant anxiety and political turmoil had strained an already delicate system. The New England trip nearly killed him. At the end of his visit to Boston, the president collapsed and had to be rushed back to Washington. For forty-eight hours his life hung in the balance. He rallied once again, but at sixty-six, his recuperative powers were declining steadily.

In the course of an otherwise innocent flattery, Van Buren referred to the aura of urgency that came to dominate the president's attitude toward the Bank. "This Bank Matter is to be the great *finale* of your public life," the vice-president observed. Convinced that he would not live out his term, Jackson mobilized all his remaining energies for a final assault on the Bank. In so doing, he gave up any thought of restructuring the party at least until he had completed his attack. Jackson was no longer content with the veto. He wanted some more potent weapon to punish the unholy alliance of nullifiers and Bank men that had turned Congress against him.

The president did not shrink from a fight with Congress. In the spring of 1833 the legislature had declared the Second Bank a safe depository of federal funds. Jackson refused to accept such a declaration, believing that the Bank had purchased this legislative goodwill and that he was duty-bound to save the congressmen from their own greedy impulses and the people from their own corrupt legislators. The president therefore informed his cabinet in March 1833 that when Congress assembled the following December, he wanted to propose creation of a new government bank, one restricted to operation in the District of Columbia. Pending the passage of enabling legislation, Jackson wanted government deposits removed from the Second Bank and placed in state banks.

Pragmatic counselors soon turned this ambitious scheme to political advantage. Again, Kendall assumed a dominant position. He cared little for the plan for a new government bank. No doubt he realized the difficulty of persuading Congress that such an institution would not enlarge presidential power. He hoped to strengthen the party in other ways. In a system of carefully regulated state banks, Kendall saw a potent political force. By removing government deposits and placing them in state institutions, Jackson "would weaken if not destroy a powerful enemy and raise up powerful friends." Kendall and his ally Reuben Whitney wanted to turn this friendship to personal as well as partisan advantage. Attorney General Roger B. Taney supported these efforts, expecting to advance in presidential esteem.

Kendall's bold proposals created further turmoil in an administration already plagued by internal dissension. Secretary of the Treasury Louis McLane, long a supporter of the Bank, sent the president a lengthy statement arguing against removal. In this instance McLane's verbosity was exceeded only by his political impotence. He had already agreed to relinquish his fiscal post so that he might become secretary of state.

Vice-president Martin Van Buren posed the most immediate obstacle to Kendall's plans. By the summer of 1833, the "heir" was not as "apparent" as he had been the previous year. With Webster waiting in the wings, Van Buren had to proceed cautiously lest the succession drama turn into a personal tragedy. He fully realized that the removal of deposits would scotch the entente with Webster. Still, Van Buren hesitated to endorse Kendall's plans, knowing that the administration could ill-afford to act without consulting Congress. He therefore urged that Jackson remove the deposits, if he must, but to do so only after Congress convened in December 1833. Characteristically, Van Buren accompanied his advice with cloying praise: "I know of no man in the purity of whose intention . . . I have greater, if as great confidence."

Jackson would have neither flattery nor delay. He had just learned of Coffee's death and feared for his own life. He wanted to strike this final blow before he died. "It is a duty I owe my country, my conscience and my God," Jackson proclaimed. Furthermore, he wanted assurances that his successor would not defile this final monument to virtue. Consequently Jackson subjected Van Buren to the crudest kind of political pressure. "It is already hinted that you are opposed to the removal of deposits, and of course privately a friend of the Bank. *This must be removed or it will do us both much harm.*" Jackson equated criticism of removal with friendship toward the Bank. He left no room for opposition on grounds of constitutional principle, respect for congressional prerogative, or even political expediency. Those who criticized removal were Biddle's tools and Jackson's enemies. Presented with such personal arguments, Van Buren had little choice but to relent. Renewal of the Bank War was at least preferable to continuation of the crusade against Southern extremism.

By removing the government deposits before the legislature convened, by presenting congressmen with a fiscal fait accompli, the president hoped to frustrate any move to recharter the Bank. The boldness of this strategy alone indicates the absence of Democratic discipline. Jackson could not rely upon Democratic control of congressional committees. He had to shock his followers to gain their attention, much as he once had to threaten mutinous militiamen to prevent wholesale desertion. Despite such tactics, Jackson did not conceive of himself as the aggressor. Throughout the spring and summer of 1833, he believed that he was acting on the defensive. To maintain that belief, he needed the cooperation of the secretary of the treasury, who would order the actual transfer of deposits.

The president thought he had a willing agent. In December 1832, he had decided to promote Louis McLane to secretary of state and be rid of the "federal leavan" that had given rise to so much fiscal confusion. To succeed McLane as secretary of the treasury, Jackson chose William J. Duane, a political nonentity thought to be a staunch opponent of the Bank. Preoccupied with the nullification crisis, the president did not solicit Duane's views on the Bank nor did he keep his prospective counselor informed on the crucial cabinet deliberations concerning the removal of deposits. Upon taking office, Duane was shocked to discover that he had been commissioned to destroy the Bank. His annoyance mounted as Amos Kendall and Reuben Whitney casually went about establishing a state bank deposit system. Duane had Jackson's word that these activities were merely precautionary, that the secretary was free to make up his mind. Assurances were cheap in the summer of 1833 and plentiful, too, as plentiful as the presidential entreaties that accumulated on Duane's desk. Evidence of the Bank's iniquity, citations of constitutional precedent, lengthy political discourse, fawning flattery—none of these moved Duane.

By September 1833, Jackson found himself in the thick of a genuine constitutional crisis. He summoned the cabinet on September 17 and played out his own peculiar version of the deliberative process. First, he announced his intention to remove the deposits, then he asked for advice. After receiving objections from a majority of the cabinet, none of which surprised him, Jackson dismissed his counselors, ordering them to appear the next day to receive his decision. The second meeting turned out to be more regal audience than council of state. There was no discussion; Jackson simply reiterated his intentions and then subjected his cabinet to a lengthy diatribe against the Bank. Prepared nearly two months previously, this polemic clearly indicated that Jackson went into these meetings with a closed mind.

Nevertheless, the president truly wanted the support of his counselors and especially Duane. He pleaded with the secretary of the treasury to formally order the removals or to resign. Duane demurred, asking two days to reach a decision. The president could not wait; he had already arranged for the *Washington Globe* to announce removal the next day. When the *Globe's* notice appeared, Duane refused to carry out the order or to resign. There followed an emotional confrontation during which Duane reminded Jackson of the constitutional duties of the secretary of the treasury and Jackson responded with a lecture on the loyalty becoming a subordinate. Neither man budged. On September 23, 1833, the president ended the impasse by formally removing Duane from office, replacing him with Roger B. Taney, the only cabinet member firmly committed to the immediate removal of the deposits.

The duel was over. Jackson left the field confident that his removal policies protected both personal and national honor. "This movement which was thought by some of my friends would destroy me, works *well*. My conscience told me it was right to stop the career of this corrupting monster. I took the step fearlessly, believing it a duty I owed my God and my country." As for Duane, Jackson consigned him to the same oblivion that he reserved for all his fallen opponents. "The business of the Treasury is progressing as tho Mr. Duane had never been born." But of course Duane had been born, and born a traitor in Jackson's eyes, a "secrete agent of the Bank" sent to "disclose the cabinet results for its benefit." Jackson was convinced that he had "caught a tartar in disguise" and therefore rid the government of one more evil agent.

In the first favorable responses to removal Jackson saw the final reward for his years of anguish and self-sacrifice. The Bank had given him no alternative but to act independently of Congress. With Biddle able to sway votes and control the press, the president believed he had to strike quickly to cripple any attempt to recharter the Bank. Having done so, he stepped back to admire his handiwork. The opposition would now have to force a restoration of deposits or introduce another recharter bill. Either tactic would provide further proof of the Bank's corrupt influence. By removing the deposits, Jackson had identified the enemy and had drawn the battle lines clearly. He felt relieved and vindicated. "Providence smiles upon the act," he said after reading the initial newspaper comments on removal, "and all the virtuous of the land sustains it. I wish you to preserve it and file it at home," he told his son. "The History of my administration will be read with interest years after I am dead and I trust will be the means of perpetuating our happy union." His countrymen were already reading the history of the administration. Far from bringing happiness and union, Jackson's actions helped perpetuate vituperation and discord.

Such was the atmosphere as Congress assembled for what would prove to be one of the most turbulent sessions in its history. A financial contraction contrived by Nicholas Biddle created widespread economic dislocation and focused public attention on the nation's capital. In Washington, confusion reigned. Jackson's critics could not believe their good fortune. Democratic forces were in disarray, and the president refused to entertain suggestions that he change his stand. "Were all the worshippers of the Golden Calf to memorialize me and request a restoration of Deposits, I would cut my right hand from my body before I would do such an act." "I am not in any Panic," he claimed. Indeed he was not. His anger was of a cold, calculating kind. In a sense, the president welcomed the criticism for it confirmed his suspicions about the Bank's political activity and justified retaliation. He was alleged to have told a group of quavering congressmen who rushed to him with reports of an impending protest march on Washington: "Gentlemen, I shall be glad to see this federal mob on Capitol Hill. I will fix their heads on the iron palisades around the square to assist your deliberations."

The opposition was not cowed by such macabre threats, but it was confused. Critics recognized Jackson's predicament but could not agree how to capitalize on it. By removing the deposits without consulting Congress, the president undermined what little remaining discipline Democrats might have mustered against the Bank. Even Jackson's supporters admitted that removal flaunted executive prerogative and challenged congressional control of financial affairs. Had Clay been able to discipline his supporters, he might have secured passage of a recharter bill, much as he had won his compromise tariff. That victory, however, had come under threat of civil war. While Clay could argue that Jackson was a tyrant, he could not show that the removal of deposits placed the nation in peril. Nor could the Kentuckian force his followers into line behind any specific fiscal legislation. His coalition was too new, too inexperienced, too unruly.

Instead of rallying under the Bank's banner, Clay, Calhoun, and Webster took turns railing against the president. The

Kentuckian began the broadside early in December 1833 by introducing resolutions denouncing the removals and censuring the president for exceeding his constitutional powers. For the next three months the Senate galleries were treated to an incredible display of forensic fireworks. Clay took a day to assail Jackson; Benton took four to reply. Webster invoked; Calhoun shrilled; Forsyth postured; all tried to cast their emotions in that high-flown rhetoric that struck one foreign observer as "full of eagles, star spangled banners, sovereign people, claptrap, flattery and humbug." Pomposity piled on pomposity, allusion on allusion, slander on slander, threat on threat, until with voices hoarse, tempers frayed, and nerves shattered, the senators voted their will.

On March 28, 1834, by a margin of eight votes, the upper house formally censured Andrew Jackson for executive excess. Then for good measure, the Senators rejected Roger B. Taney as secretary of the treasury. If "Clay, Calhoun and Co." designed their jeremiads to provoke the president's wrath, then they certainly succeeded. By the time the Senate voted, Jackson had worked himself into a frenzy. He continually complained of being surrounded "with hypocrites and false friends, with the daily slanders and abuse of my political enemies"; he complained, too, about constant ill health. "I have this morning put on a medicated Hare skin," he said of his latest home remedy, "with the hare next the skin." Given the President's erratic spelling, it is unclear whether he was indulging some penchant for furs or practicing medieval medicine. Certainly he wanted to drive out the senatorial devils who had so tormented him during the session. "The storm in Congress is still raging," he told his son, "Clay reckless and full of fury as a drunken man in a brothel." Jackson claimed that Clay's "abuse and his coadjutors pass harmless by me." Far from passing him by, the senatorial censure brought forth one of the most spirited state papers ever to issue from the White House.

True to its author's character, the president's "Protest" was furious, contradictory, and intensely personal, combining constitutional theory, partisan rhetoric, and imperious indignation into an impassioned defense of the man and the office. For fully half of this lengthy message, Jackson excoriated the Senate's misuse of impeachment powers, even pointing out that the censure resolution was not legitimate legislation because the House had not given its assent. Instead of developing a crisp, consistent attack, Jackson belabored the impeachment issue, approaching it from every conceivable direction. He did so out of frustration, for as he admitted in the protest, the Senate censure was "too general and indefinite to be easily repelled, but yet sufficiently precise to bring into discredit the conduct and motives of the executive." Jackson was prepared to defend that conduct in person. "Oh, if I live to get these robes of office off me," he said during Clay's assault, "I will bring that rascal to dear account." Jackson would have preferred impeachment to censure, for then he would have been able to confront his accusers face to face. The Senate action denied him the opportunity.

He could only protest verbally and in the most personal terms. Near the close of his message, Jackson expressed his deep sense of outrage and injury. He portrayed himself alternately as dutiful public servant, self-sacrificing war hero, and assailed executive. He proclaimed:

Never in the fire of youth nor in the vigor of manhood could I find an attraction to lure me from the path of duty, and now I shall scarcely find an inducement to commence their career of ambition when gray hairs and a decaying frame, instead of inviting me to toil and battle call me to the contemplation of other worlds, where conquerers cease to be honored and usurpers expiate their crimes.

Grant him the strength, he asked God, grant him the support, he asked the people, and he hoped to "heal the wounds of the constitution and preserve it from further violation." This done, he would "die contented with the belief that I have contributed in some small degree to increase the value and prolong the duration of American liberty."

Powerful, the protest was also politically astute. As they had done so effectively in 1828, party leaders submerged their differences and asked the voters to rally behind the "decaying frame" of the Old Hero, to protect him from assault. By claiming that the Senate had usurped the power of impeachment, they parried charges that Jackson had usurped the power of the purse. By assailing the monstrous corruption of Biddle's Bank, Democrats deflected attacks on the new "pet banks" in which the president had placed the government deposits. These effective appeals coupled with a return of economic prosperity enabled the Democratic party to regain some strength in the 1834 congressional elections.

Still, at the state level, the Jackson coalition showed definite signs of strain. The most serious defections came in Virginia, long considered a key Democratic stronghold. Under the leadership of John Tyler, discontented state-rights advocates exploited the nullification crisis and the removal controversy; in 1834, they handed the Richmond Junto its first major defeat. A similar revolt flared in North Carolina, where former cabinet member John Branch lent his name to the campaign against executive usurpation. In Pennsylvania, the removal of deposits spurred the Bank's supporters to stage a lengthy battle in the state legislature and gave rise to a new party organization that adopted the name "Whig," a label in great vogue among Jackson's opponents. For the president, the most cruel blow came in his home state of Tennessee, where a movement was underway to run Hugh Lawson White for president. Begun with the assumption that Jackson would welcome the candidacy of his old friend, the campaign soon became a full-fledged revolt as the president denounced White in the most uncomplimentary terms.

Jackson could not use the power of the presidency to halt these defections. He entered office as the head of a decentral-

ized, state-oriented coalition, pledged to simplify public administration and return power to the people. He could not
establish greater central control of the party, not without raising doubts about his commitment to maintain state sovereignty, as he discovered during the nullification crisis.
Democrats applauded Jackson's vigorous use of the veto, because the veto curbed centralized power and promoted state
activism. So, too, they accepted the removal of deposits because this action benefited state banks and reduced the possibility that a corrupt national government, under Bank
influence, might endanger state interests. Nevertheless,
Democrats balked at giving the president too much power.
Jackson was able to withdraw the deposits and place them in
state banks, but he was never able to establish firm control
over his "pets." By 1836, the administration was forced to
issue the Specie Circular, a tacit admission that the deposit
system had fostered inflation and irresponsible banking.

To control the activities of independent state machines just
as to manage the affairs of state banks, the president needed
a bureaucracy and communications system far more extensive
than custom or technology would allow. Jackson spoke often
of a new direction in public administration, but the words rang
hollow. Congress repeatedly wreaked havoc with his appointments, destroying all chances of instituting the policy of rotation in office. What limited patronage powers the president
did possess he often had to share with state politicians. With
a miniscule personal staff and a cabinet that displayed more
animosity than harmony, Jackson lacked the personnel to create a national party organization. Informal advisors like Lewis
and Kendall carried out executive directives, but they were
overworked and forced to bear the brunt of congressional
attacks. The *Washington Globe* proved an uncertain trumpet. Its
circulation never exceeded a few thousand copies. Blair labored for years without congressional patronage. As a consequence, the *Globe* was often in financial straits. For all its access
to the administration, Blair's journal remained provincial in

scope, vying with other influential state presses for political backing. High yearly subscription rates put the *Globe* out of reach of the common man.

None of this inherent weakness disturbed Andrew Jackson. He had no intention of creating a powerful national party. Throughout his presidency, he retained a low opinion of politics and politicians. Believing both corrupt, he felt fully justified in seeking revenge against his political enemies, but always in the name of honor, never in the pursuit of institutional development or party unity. Politics offered him a means of achieving vindication, nothing more, nothing less. The Democratic coalition unconsciously endorsed such a personal mission. With Andrew Jackson's character at issue in many elections, the party could deemphasize national problems likely to breed dissension. Under the comfortable rubric of state rights and military heroism, Democratic politicians were free to appeal to the voters in the language of local custom.

This appeal began to wear thin as Jackson's presidency wore on. Democrats could still win with the politics of ballyhoo and heroism, but the Whigs had gained an important foothold in the states. They needed only a presidential candidate who could pose as the true Cincinnatus, come to rescue the government from a crazed imposter. When the Democratic convention selected Martin Van Buren as its presidential candidate in May 1835, Whig prospects seemed brighter. For one thing, the nomination put an end to fears that Jackson might seek a third term. Furthermore, the Whigs could easily charge the Democrats with bowing to the will of the dictator, secretly rejoicing all the while that the new Democratic standard-bearer bore little resemblance to any known variety of *heroicus Americanus.* Prospects they had aplenty; the Whigs needed only agreement.

Just when the Democratic coalition seemed to be tottering, good fortune allowed the administration to make some emergency repairs. In the summer and fall of 1835, the American Anti-Slavery Society inaugurated a new, aggressive propaganda campaign, flooding the Southern mails with tracts and pamphlets. A substantial amount of this literature reached its destination, where nervous postmasters coped as best they could. In Charleston, on July 30, 1835, a mob burned the offensive mail and hung abolitionists in effigy. The president deplored the violence, deplored too the incendiary tracts that preached rebellion. Constitutionally pledged to protect the sanctity of the mails, he could do little to prevent dispatch of such material. But through his new postmaster general Amos Kendall, Jackson let it be known that he would not interfere should local postmasters take the Constitution into their own hands and destroy the abolitionist tracts. Jackson even suggested that postmasters keep a record of any Southerner who subscribed to such documents so that local justice might run its course. By aiding and abetting Southern politicians in their battle against the abolitionists, Jackson helped curb Whig inroads in the South. The administration's covert assistance came as a welcome relief from the aggressive policies of the nullification crisis. Not since the Bank veto had the president so ably upheld state rights.

This was a small triumph, not the sort that would endear Andrew Jackson to posterity or repay the Senate for its insult. As the days of his final term dwindled in number, the president had a restless look in his eye, as though eager for one last battle. He despaired of achieving immortality through his adopted son. Andrew Jackson, Jr., was an increasing embarrassment, his personal finances in constant disrepair, his drinking habits the cause of considerable alarm. The president preached, he lectured, he threatened—all to no apparent avail. In this gathering twilight, Jackson clung to one final hope, turning his attention to faraway Texas, where a revolution was brewing under the leadership of Tennessee's Sam Houston, a man the president often treated like a son.

Jackson rarely took such a personal interest in foreign policy as he took in Texas. Normally, he allowed his secretaries of state great latitude. Van Buren, Livingston, McLane, and John Forsyth handled the routine matters of state with dispatch and made significant advances: reopening the West Indies trade, reparations from Denmark and Spain, and a commercial treaty with Turkey. In the few minor crises of his presidency, Jackson reacted with caution and restraint. When England extended sovereignty over the Falkland Islands in 1833, the president did not protest even though the action violated the Monroe Doctrine. He was too busy combatting disunion at home to worry about a minor incident abroad. While relations with England remained placid, negotiations with France nearly erupted into naval hostilities, owing in large part to Jackson's delicate sense of honor.

The confrontation between the United States and France grew out of a long-standing claims dispute. On July 4, 1831, France finally agreed to pay twenty-five million francs for damages inflicted on American shipping during the Napoleonic wars. Because this payment was bound to raise taxes and incur public displeasure, the French ministry delayed introduction of the necessary enabling legislation. The Jackson administration had precipitously issued a draft for the first installment and was chagrined when the request came back with a notice of insufficient funds. That Nicholas Biddle handled the fiscal negotiations and charged the Treasury both penalty and interest added to the president's mounting displeasure.

Throughout the spring and summer of 1834, Jackson agonized over the proper response to the repeated French delays. He ordered the Navy placed on alert and considered asking Congress for permission to issue Letters of Marque and Reprisal—a virtual declaration of naval warfare. Once again, Van Buren tried to serve as peacemaker; he dissuaded the president from such aggressive measures, but he could not alter the tone of the annual message. Jackson assailed French intransigence and suggested that French property be seized should the stalemate continue. Although Congress refused to be a party to such bullying, the message had its desired effect. In the spring of 1835, the French Chamber of Deputies yielded, but it perversely made payment contingent on an explanation of the offensive tone in the president's message. At this, Jackson flew into yet another towering rage. Nearly six months elapsed before Jackson's ire cooled sufficiently and intermediaries achieved a peaceful settlement.

The president's counselors were powerless in negotiations with Mexico. From the outset of his administration, Jackson insisted on controlling the destiny of his beloved Southwest. He considered himself an expert in frontier diplomacy, especially that involving areas once under his military command. The defender of New Orleans remained convinced that the Mississippi was the commercial lifeline of the country and that further territorial acquisition would protect this strategic artery against foreign aggrandizement. In particular he coveted the Mexican province of Texas. Jackson regretted that in 1819 the United States had relinquished claim to this prize in order to acquire Florida. Other Americans shared his appetite. Nearly 20,000 of them migrated to the promising territory by 1830, creating the beginnings of what would soon become an entrenched system of plantation slavery. These settlers chafed under Mexican rule and eagerly awaited the day when they could attach themselves to their parent country.

Prejudice played no small part in Jackson's dealings with Mexico. He considered Mexicans inferior and incapable of establishing a stable social order. Instead of lauding the revolutionary movement that put an end to Spanish rule, Jackson believed that ferment "hostile to us—opposed to the conclusion of those commercial regulations which the interest of both countries calls for. . . ." Jackson contended that Mexicans would be perpetually "setting up and pulling down rulers," and therefore had no right to deny Texans the benefit of democratic rule. In 1830, when he made these observations, the president perceived his own society in a state of moral decay. The establishment of stability in Texas therefore took on as much importance as the creation of an Indian civilization west of the Mississippi.

Jackson's Mexican diplomacy stemmed directly from his experience as frontier general and treaty commissioner. Having long regarded Indians as wayward children who responded only to venality and violence, Jackson transferred these prejudices to the Mexicans, many of whom were, in fact, of Indian descent. Mexicans, too, had more territory than they could use. "Not yet placed in a situation by the harmony, intelligence and number of her citizens, to regard extent of territory, as we do, an important agent in the development and preservation of the Representative principle, she must be sensible that it is in truth the vital source of her weakness." Jackson was willing to help remedy that vital weakness by purchasing a large portion of northern Mexico. If the Mexicans would not listen to reason, Jackson had no compunctions about resorting to bribery. "I scarcely ever knew a Spaniard who was not the slave of avarice," the president said at the outset of negotiations to purchase Texas, "and it is not *improbable* that this *weakness* may be *worth a great deal to us, in this case.*" This assessment matched Jackson's earlier conclusion that "avarice and fear are the predominant passions that govern an Indian." Having frightened the Indians into submission, Jackson assumed that similar tactics would work with Mexicans. Of course the United States would never invade Texas, but Jackson thought the day might come when Mexican instability would "compel us in self defense to seize that country by force and establish a regular government, *there* over it."

Jackson chose Anthony Butler as minister to Mexico in disregard of diplomatic protocol. The president wanted an agent he could trust, and so he selected a personal favorite with practically no qualifications for the post. That Butler claimed land in an area he hoped to wrest from Mexico constituted no conflict of interest to Jackson. In his original letter of instructions, issued in the fall of 1829, the president set the tone for a relationship that lasted for the next six years. Butler was to ingratiate himself with "the President of Mexico, or other high functionaries of that Government" by *"very confidentially"* showing them his private instructions from the State Department. Actually this involved no risk since these formal instructions made no mention of Texas. Jackson calculated that the mere act of disclosure, accompanied by hushed requests for absolute confidentiality, would stand the new minister in good stead.

After executing this artifice, Butler was to proceed with the business of buying Texas. Jackson was willing to pay $5 million for the new province—willing, too, for Butler to facilitate the purchase by judicious bribes to Mexican officials. Judicious to Jackson meant undercover. He always hinted at such payments, never mentioned them directly, but he knew full well that Butler would propose them. Mexican officials turned aside these overtures, pointing out that their new Constitution forbade any such cessions. Undaunted, Jackson continued to urge Butler on, sending him coded messages with reminders of the *"great importance of the cession of Texas to us in maintaining future peace and good neighborhood between the United States and Mexico."*

By the beginning of his second term, the president began to reevaluate his agent's utility. Not that Butler's notorious private life, his sexual peccadilloes, land speculations, filibustering, or loan-sharking caused Jackson alarm. The president had tolerated greater vices in more important men. Butler committed the cardinal sin of breaking the confidentiality of correspondence. In October 1833, he wrote Jackson an extremely indiscreet letter, mentioning the president's authorization of bribes. It was bad enough that Butler referred to such a matter, worse still that he failed to encode his remarks, and positively outrageous that his frank statements should arrive by regular mail at the very moment when the administration's political enemies were gathering in Congress to assail the removal of deposits from the Bank. The letter was not intercepted. It arrived safely and remained in Jackson's possession. Butler remained on duty in Mexico, but the relationship was never the same. The president continued to press for the purchase of Texas; at the same time he was prepared to make Butler the scapegoat if the details of the sale ever came into question.

Revolution put an end to these covert transactions. In the fall of 1835, with the help of a substantial number of American volunteers, Texans declared their independence and took up arms against Mexico. Jackson had reason to rejoice at this turn of events. The rebellion might well save the United States $5 million. He could also derive vicarious satisfaction from the exploits of his protégé, Sam Houston, commander of the Texas forces.

Of all the president's personal favorites, Houston had led the most colorful and controversial life. As an aspiring thespian in an amateur Nashville theatrical, Houston once drew praise for his ability to "assume the ludicrous or the sublime." His career vacillated wildly between these extremes. From an untutored youth spent in part among the Indians, he rose to become governor of Tennessee, only to resign in 1829 when his new marriage disintegrated. He went back to live among the Indians. The Cherokees always had found Houston's appetites remarkable. As a boy they called him The Raven, as a man, The Big Drunk. The president tolerated such excess, trained Houston for duels, cheered his assault on a member of Congress, supported his designs to profit on Indian removal, and listened to his plans for Texas.

When the news of Houston's victory at San Jacinto reached Washington in the spring of 1836, Jackson rejoiced but, curiously, that was all he did. Although Southern newspapers urged the immediate recognition of the new regime, the president demurred. Political realities tempered his enthusiasm. With Van Buren trying to keep the issue out of the campaign, with abolitionists threatening an uproar at the mere discussion of annexing new slave territory, and with Congress about to adjourn, even the most rabid Texas partisan could see that delay was politic. Much as he considered himself a realistic man, Jackson had other, more personal reasons for deferring to the dictates of party unity.

The president wanted Texas, but on his own terms. Purchase was preferable to revolution. But for Butler's "delay and misconduct Texas would have belonged to this *Government* before the war broke out," he said later. What spineless congressman would have objected to a transaction that purchased both strategic territory and Mexican good will? By contrast, revolution raised a host of problems. As president, Jackson was bound to honor American neutrality, a duty at odds with his private sympathies. Much as he wanted to give military assistance to the new republic, he could not do so without violating treaty obligations to Mexico and instigating a war that by no stretch of the imagination would be in self-defense. Most of all, the rebellion robbed Jackson of control. The president could not manipulate a revolutionary regime any more than he could create order out of congressional chaos. The Battle of San Jacinto diminished the chance that Jackson could present Texas to the nation before his presidency ran its term.

There was so little time now, less than six months. Martin Van Buren had won election over the Whigs, who had been unable to decide on a single candidate and instead ran several. The president-elect was busily engaged in forming his cabinet. Congress was preparing to assemble, and the incessant round of charges and counter-charges promised to begin anew. For a while, Jackson thought of making a fight over Texas. Freed by the election from obligations to party, he might yet pit his personal popularity against the congressional opposition.

The spirit may have been willing but the flesh was pitifully weak. Late in November 1836, Jackson collapsed again. For days anxious relatives hovered over his gaunt, pale figure. Doctors drew nearly sixty ounces of blood to alleviate the hemorrhaging. Politicians drew promises that a healthy Jackson might never have made. On December 21, 1836, Congress received the president's special report on the subject of Texas recognition. No bold new declaration here, merely a pale replica of his earlier pronouncements. The will to fight was rapidly fading. Jackson told Congress to wrestle with the delicate problem of recognition; Van Buren privately rejoiced.

Suddenly in February 1837, the old fire returned. Stung by a congressional investigation that called even his military reputation into question, Jackson abandoned his pacific policies toward Mexico. There was no time to press for annexation of Texas; Jackson would have to be content to recognize the new regime on his last day in office. But there was still time to lash out at Mexican instability, to make one last symbolic defense of order and discipline.

The pretext was a festering claims dispute nearly a decade old. On February 6, 1837, the president formally notified Congress that he had lost all patience with the Mexicans. Their constant delays and diplomatic insults "would justify in the eyes of all nations immediate war." "Considering the present embarrassed condition of that country," Jackson urged Congress to "act with moderation and wisdom by giving to Mexico one more opportunity to atone for the past." The president wanted this final demand delivered from the decks of an American warship, and he asked Congress to grant him authority to initiate naval reprisals should Mexican intransigence persist. This belligerent message really had little to do with Mexico. While trying to pressure Mexico into a settlement, Jackson was also trying to protect his reputation from congressional assault. By asking for another force bill, he hoped to compel his critics to kneel once more at the altar of martial authority. There would be no surrender on Capitol Hill, however, only maneuvers, delays, and polite refusals. No heroic appeal, no call to arms could rally forces that now looked to a new leader.

His health shattered, his enemies relentless, his character still in question, Andrew Jackson desperately wanted a final reckoning. The people might judge him "more impartially," he thought, "in quitting public life" than they had in the past. Following the example of the country's greatest general and political sage, Jackson decided to issue a Farewell Address "as a means of rendering a last service to my country." The address served Jackson as well. In assessing the state of the Union, the president was trying, as he put it, "to impress upon my countrymen the true scope of all my efforts." Inevitably, the address told the tale of injured innocence at war with the forces of corruption. Beware, Jackson lectured his public, of "enemies who often assume the disguise of friends." Jackson knew them well; "I have devoted the last hours of my public life to warn you of that danger."

The bright sunshine, the noisy crowds, the martial music drowned out these solemn admonitions. Against his doctor's orders, the president joined the inaugural procession that wound its way slowly to Capitol Hill. There in the presence of his enemies, Jackson fully intended to savor his revenge. Chief Justice Roger B. Taney, once rejected as secretary of the treasury, would administer the oath of office to Martin Van Buren, once refused appointment as minister to England. The ceremony was brief. In his inaugural address, President Van Buren paid homage to his predecessor. "For him I but express with my own the wishes of all, that he may yet long live to enjoy the brilliant evening of his well spent life." The inaugural was over. As Jackson descended the steps of the platform, the huge crowd broke into a deafening cheer that reverberated down Pennsylvania Avenue. However sweet, the moment was but a small reward for all the slander, the insult, the pain. Only a moment, it passed too quickly.

IX

"I Am Dying as Fast as I Can"

THE JOURNEY TO THE HERMITAGE renewed Jackson's faith in his own rectitude. "I have been everywhere cheered by my numerous democratic republican friends," the Old Hero proudly reported. Even some "repenting Whigs" joined in giving him "a hearty welcome." Jackson felt vindicated. "When I review the arduous administration thro' which I have passed, the formidable opposition I have met to its very close, by the combined talents, wealth and power of the whole aristocracy of the Union . . . the result must not only be pleasing to me but to every patriot." Eight years of intrigue and confrontation had only reinforced Jackson's egocentric view of the political process. At his inauguration, upon his retirement, he assumed that the people were a mighty army come to vanquish his enemies. "It was the sovereign people that nobly sustained me against this formidable power and enabled me to terminate my administration so satisfactorily. . . ." Everywhere, Jackson heard the cries " 'well done thou faithful servant.' " "This is truly the patriot's reward, and a source of great gratification to me, and will be a solace to the grave."

In a sense, the Democrats were an army marching at his call, not to defend ideology, but to combat corruption. Jackson's emotions, not his principles, commanded their allegiance and determined the structure of the party. Distrustful of politics and politicians, Andrew Jackson made little attempt to strengthen the central party organization or to make it subservient to the executive branch. As president, he increased neither the size of the federal bureaucracy nor the martial establishment. He never institutionalized the policy of rotation in office, except in his cabinet where the constant turnover detracted from the formation of consistent policy. In his battles with Congress, Jackson appealed for public sympathy but rarely for legislative discipline. "The veto works well," he said so often; but it did not work well, not as a means of managing Congress, not even as a defense of executive prerogatives. For if Andrew Jackson made the presidency more visible, he also made it more vulnerable to charges of executive usurpation, and this worked to the detriment of party unity. But then, to Jackson, party unity was of secondary importance. He spent most of his eight years in Washington defending himself against real and imaginary enemies. His sense of honor and mission would let him do no less; the structure of the democracy encouraged him to do no more.

While chafing at his boldness and impetuosity, the party accepted Jackson's personal leadership. With the hero in power and heroism the issue in many elections, Democrats could avoid internal divisions so natural and costly in an age of growing sectional tensions. Once the hero retired, the party ceased to prosper.

The new president did not trade on the reputation of the old. Jackson's heroic image had no organizational grounding. Van Buren might retain Old Hickory's trusted advisors, but he could not duplicate the general's style, nor did he try. Instead the Red Fox went his own way, maintaining cordial relations with his predecessor but rarely soliciting his advice on major matters of domestic or foreign policy. "A party of principles, not men," this was the new professional creed that governed Van Buren as a politician and as a president.

Prolonged economic depression soon put both creed and politician to the test. In reacting to the Panic of 1837, Van Buren proposed that Congress create a sub-Treasury system, thereby removing government funds from failing state banks. For the next three years debate on this measure dragged on, revealing the inherent weakness of the Democratic coalition, weakness hitherto partially hidden by prosperity and by the appeal of Jackson's martial feats. By asking his followers to abandon state banks and support a sub-Treasury, Van Buren forced them to choose between state and national interest. The Democratic alliance rested on the assumption that the two would always be in harmony, that adherence to the principle of limited government would protect state rights. The sub-Treasury expanded the power of the central government. Van Buren won his battle but only after extended internecine warfare that destroyed Democratic unity.

Jackson never lost interest in these matters, only influence. Like Cincinnatus, he had returned to the plow; he might offer advice and comment but custom prevented a more active role in party affairs. Much as he had dreamed of a peaceful retirement, Jackson grew restive at the Hermitage. Plantation management consumed his time and failing energies but brought little emotional reward. He found it difficult to take pride in his material estate when his heir was proving a spendthrift.

By 1840, Jackson feared for his political legacy as well. The Whigs had selected their own rustic hero, William Henry Harrison, to oppose Van Buren's bid for reelection. Democrats needed an innovative strategy to counter this challenge and alleviate public dismay over the lingering financial crisis. Jackson wanted to be of service, but he seemed more concerned about his party's standing in Tennessee than in the nation. Throughout the spring and summer of 1840 he tried in vain to prevent vice-president Richard M. Johnson from running for a second term, insisting that Tennessee's James K. Polk would attract more western votes. The vice-president's adherents argued that, of all people, Jackson should appreciate the political value of martial exploits. For as the Democratic campaign ditty so proudly proclaimed: "Rumpsey, Dumpsey, Colonel Johnson shot Tecumseh."

Jackson was distressed by this new direction in politics, insensitive to its origins in his own presidential campaigns. He ridiculed Harrison and refused to believe that the voters would actually respond to the "hum bugery" of "coons, big balls and hard cider." Such feelings protected Jackson against the unthinkable: that in 1828 the voters might actually have rallied to the side of heroism in general rather than his heroics in particular. By denying Old Tippecanoe any legitimate claim on public sufferages, Old Hickory preserved his own sense of rectitude. Jackson soon fell back on this self-righteousness as the Whigs carried the presidential election of 1840 by a wide margin. "The democracy of the United States has been shamefully beaten," Jackson admitted, "but I trust *not conquered.* I still hope there is sufficient virtue in the unbought people of this union, to stay the perjury, bribery, fraud and imposition upon the people by the vilest system of slander that ever before existed, even in the most corrupt days of Ancient Rome."

Convinced that conspiracy again ruled the Washington community, Jackson rejoiced when Harrison died less than a month after taking office. "I anticipated the result," the ex-president observed. "He had not sufficient energy to drive from him the office hunters." "A kind and overruling providence has interfered to prolong our glorious Union and happy republican system which Genl. Harrison and his cabinet were preparing to destroy." A callous postmortem perhaps, but then it came from the pen of an anxious old man who feared that providence would not prolong his own frail constitution. If, as Jackson seemed to believe, death visited the corrupt before the infirm, then he might survive a while longer, at least until his party returned to power.

Jackson survived to see the Democrats triumph in the fall of 1844, to welcome the annexation of Texas that winter, and to read of the inauguration of his favorite, James K, Polk, in March 1845. "All is safe at last," Old Hickory said; still he could not relax. He had to make up for all the years of isolation, for all the spites, the snubs, the lingering slanders, but above all for the loss of authority. Jackson pestered the president with advice about appointments—always appointments—as if by choosing the right men, "Young Hickory" would guarantee a successful administration. Polk patiently received the advice, dutifully replied and then, like Van Buren, struck out on his own.

The Old Hero had survived too long perhaps. With the Democrats returning to power, he found himself surrounded by the very supplicants whose ambition he privately loathed. "I am dying as fast as I can, and they know it, but they will keep swarming upon me in crowds seeking office—intriguing for office." He should have sent them away, for they drew more than feeble promises. They deprived him of dignity in his final days. Yet he clung to the hope that through these aspirants he could gain some influence in the new administration. Instead of deferring to these patronage requests, Polk actually discharged two of Jackson's oldest supporters: William B. Lewis and Francis P. Blair. Old Hickory wrote furious letters of protest, trying to stay the executions, but to no avail. When reason failed, when political persuasion brought only polite refusals, Jackson threatened the president with the only weapon still remaining. "My whole system, a jelly," Jackson wrote less than two weeks before his death. "You can run a finger half an inch into the limb and the impression will remain for minutes—added to this I have a bowel complaint upon me, a difficulty in urinating & a severe attack of piles."

By early June 1845, Jackson knew the decay was irreversible. The pain persisted, but suddenly the agony of doubt was gone. He was convinced now that death would come and bring the peace, the reckoning that a life of controversy denied him. On Sunday, June 8, the slaves gathered in front of the mansion chanting softly in the warm summer air. The old man heard the mourning and whispered calmly, "Oh do not cry. Be good children, and we shall all meet in heavan."

Death brought peace; time has brought vindication. Honored in his own day for martial heroism, Andrew Jackson now symbolizes presidential greatness. Founder of the national party system, champion of the common man, and creator of the strong presidency are but a few of the accolades history and historians accord him. Jackson did not set out to serve these ends. His goals were more limited, more personal. Yet in waging war against his enemies, in defending his reputation against assault, and in trying to restore virtue to government, he displayed a vigor and a determination that captured the attention of his fellow citizens and the acclaim of the ages.

A Note on the Sources

MOST OF ANDREW JACKSON'S personal papers are in the Library of Congress and are available on microfilm. The Tennessee State Library and the Ladies Hermitage Society have additional material on Old Hickory's early life as well as his presidency. Harriet C. Owsley's bibliographical article in the *Tennessee Historical Quarterly,* XXVI (Spring 1967), 97–100 describes these holdings and other pertinent collections, especially the papers of John Overton and John Coffee. Pending completion of the new project to collect and publish all extant Jackson correspondence, John S. Bassett and J. Franklin Jameson, eds., *The Correspondence of Andrew Jackson* (7 vols., Washington, D.C., 1926–1935) remains the standard compendium. The papers of Nicholas Biddle, Francis P. Blair, Andrew J. Donelson, Duff Green, Amos Kendall, James K. Polk, and Levi Woodbury—all in the Library of Congress—contain indispensable information on Jackson's candidacy and behavior as president. James D. Richardson, ed., *The Messages and Papers of the Presidents, 1789–1897* (10 vols., Washington, D.C., 1900) includes Jackson's messages to Congress.

Although this personal correspondence is illuminating, the memoirs of the Jacksonian period are singularly unenlightening. Those who stood closest to the president either left no recollections or, like Amos Kendall, chose to generalize rather than chronicle. His *Autobiography* (2 vols., Boston, 1872) briefly touches on the major controversies of Jackson's two terms but reveals little about the president's motivations. *The Autobiography of Martin Van Buren* (Washington, D.C., 1920) is much more detailed but was written at a time when its author had reason to glorify his association with Old Hickory. Similar distortion mars Thomas Hart Benton, *Thirty Years View* (2 vols., New York, 1854–1856).

Newspapers constitute the most important source for party rhetoric and provide occasional glimpses of the intricate workings of political machinery. The *Albany Argus, Nashville Union* and *Richmond Enquirer* were the Democrats' most prominent and influential state papers, while the *United States Telegraph* and the *Washington Globe* served the party in the nation's capital. For the opposition view, see the *National Intelligencer.*

Historians continue to be indebted to James Parton, whose biography of Andrew Jackson (3 vols., New York, 1861) contains so much essential source material. Apocryphal though many of Parton's stories may be, they come from men like William B. Lewis, who were close to the center of power and who left no recollections of their own. Of twentieth-century treatments, John Spencer Bassett, *The Life of Andrew Jackson* (2 vols., New York, 1911) is the most factual; Marquis James, *Andrew Jackson* (2 vols. in one, Indianapolis, 1938), the most readable; and Robert Remini, *Andrew Jackson* (New York, 1966), the most interpretive. Two essential works analyze Old Hickory as hero and Democratic figurehead: John W. Ward, *Andrew Jackson, Symbol for an Age* (New York, 1955) and Marvin Meyers, *The Jacksonian Persuasion* (Stanford, 1957). Thomas Perkins Abernathy, *From Frontier to Plantation in Tennessee* (Chapel Hill, N.C., 1932) is the best analysis of Jackson's search for social and political position in Tennessee.

Of the many fine biographies of Jackson's contemporaries, three are of special significance. Charles G. Sellers, Jr., *James K. Polk* (2 vols., Princeton, N.J., 1957–1966) illuminates early Tennessee history as well as congressional politics in the 1830s. John Munroe's exhaustive study of *Louis McLane* (New Brunswick, N.J., 1973) presents new correspondence on the Bank War and the nullification crisis. In his partisan but reliable biography of *Nicholas Biddle* (Chicago, 1959), Thomas P. Govan helps establish the critical personal dimension of the attack on the Bank.

In analyzing Jackson's behavior, I have profited from reading Robert Lifton, *Death in Life* (New York, 1967), a splendid analysis of the psychology of "survival" and an invaluable guide to other pertinent psychological literature. For a more complete, psychoanalytical portrait of Jackson, focusing on his relations with the Indians, see Michael Rogin, *Fathers and Children: Andrew Jackson and the Subjugation of the American Indian* (New York, 1975). Two treatments of frontier society help establish the cultural context of Jackson's early life. Richard M. Brown, *The South Carolina Regulators* (Cambridge, Mass., 1963) discusses the causes of back country instability, while Harriett Arnow, *Seedtime on the Cumberland* (New York, 1960) contains a wealth of information of the colonization of middle Tennessee.

The literature on Jacksonian politics and social life is voluminous and best approached through a number of fine bibliographical essays, the most recent of which is in Edward Pessen's admirable survey, *Jacksonian America* (Homewood, Ill., 1969). Pessen is particularly effective in his analysis of Arthur Schlesinger, Jr., *The Age of Jackson* (Boston, 1945) and the response to this monumental work of American historiography. James Sterling Young renders Washington politics comprehensible in *The Washington Community, 1800–1828* (New York, 1966), although he closes his excellent account with the dubious statement that Jackson's election put an end to political drift and instability. In *The Idea of a Party System* (Berkeley, Calif., 1970), Richard Hofstadter analyzes the ideology of party formation and carefully delineates the biases that Jackson and his contemporaries brought to politics. For an excellent investigation of party growth, consult Richard P. McCormick, *The Second American Party System* (Chapel Hill, N.C., 1966). By far the most penetrating study of state politics is William Freehling, *Prelude to Civil War* (New York, 1966), a superb investigation of South Carolina and the nullification crisis. Rowland Berthoff, *An Unsettled People* (New York, 1971) and David J. Rothman, *The Discovery of Asylum* (Boston, 1971) provide the best introduction to the sweeping changes that occurred in the United States during Jackson's lifetime.

On the specific issues of Jackson's presidency several works bear mention. Robert Remini, *Andrew Jackson and the Bank War* (New York, 1967) skillfully narrates this confusing conflict, although he does not supplant the partisan but magisterial work of Bray Hammond in *Banks and Politics in America* (Princeton, 1957). In *Daniel Webster and Jacksonian Democracy* (Baltimore, 1973), Sydney Nathans presents a superb analysis of Jackson's flirtation with party realignment. Mary Young, *Redskins, Ruffleshirts and Red Necks* (Norman, Okla., 1961) and Bernard Sheehan, *Seeds of Extinction* (Chapel Hill, N.C., 1973) discuss the major issues relating to Indian removal.

Index